A Young Woman's Guide to Health and Well-Being

The Pilates Handbook

A Young Woman's Guide to Health and Well-Being

The Pilates

Handbook

Roger Brignell

ROSEN
PUBLISHING®

New York

This edition published in 2010 by:

The Rosen Publishing Group, Inc.
29 East 21st Street
New York, NY 10010

Library of Congress Cataloging-in-Publication Data

Brignell, Roger.
The pilates handbook / Roger Brignell.
    p. cm.—(A young woman's guide to health and well-being)
Includes bibliographical references and index.
ISBN-13: 978-1-4358-5361-4 (library binding)
1. Pilates method—Handbooks, manuals, etc. 2. Exercise for women—
Handbooks, manuals, etc. I. Title.
RA781.4.B75 2009
613.7'192—dc22

                                                                2009010317

Manufactured in china

Contents

Introduction

Exercise and exercisers today are very different
from those of ten years ago, largely because of
the way in which exercisers have changed, in
terms of both what they want to achieve
through exercise and the kinds of programs
that they are prepared to follow.

Introduction

Anyone who reads a newspaper or watches television today cannot have failed to have noticed that there have been some significant changes in the way that exercise for both fitness and health is being talked about and practiced.

In the past, any exercise tended to be viewed as a good thing. "Fitness" and "health" were used as virtually synonymous words. (They are not: the very fit are frequently far from healthy, and sometimes suffer from overtraining, which often results in chronic injury and always results in some suppression of the immune system.) If you went to a gym or health club, it was packed with machines to help you to perform resistance exercises, as well as machines to facilitate cardiovascular training. In those

Free weights are relative newcomers to the gym.

Classes in yoga and Pilates are common.

stability balls. The class timetable is likely to focus on yoga, meditation, and Pilates, with classes like spinning and kickboxing replacing aerobics and step classes.

Gyms and health clubs operate in a very competitive business environment. They do not spend the kind of money on changing equipment and training teachers on the scale that is implied above unless they have a very good commercial reason to do so. In the fitness business, the only commercial reason that could be sufficiently large enough to drive such a change must obviously come from the

gyms that catered to the casual exerciser, you would have been hard-pressed to see free weights, these being viewed as dangerous objects likely to injure unsuspecting exercisers. The class timetable was filled with aerobics, step, and toning classes, and a Swiss ball was nowhere to be seen. In short, everything was calculated on a kind of "one-size-fits-all" basis designed to give the least risk or trouble to the provider of the facility, with the needs and requirements of the exerciser coming a poor second.

The approach today is very different. First, the gym—if it is a good one—will have far fewer machines. There will be a wide range of free-weight equipment to suit all sizes, and there will most likely be a range of medicine balls, "sit fits," and other, more specialized bits of equipment, such as

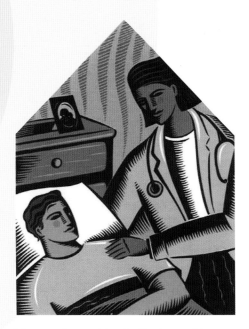

It is easy to become injured without supervision.

changing demands of the customer. But what could have happened to change what the customer requires from his or her gym?

I believe that three things combined to make this happen. First, sports' scientists produced new research that suggested that common chronic injuries were often self-inflicted, and that they could be avoided by following an exercise program that was more appropriate for the daily life of the individual. Clearly, a set of machines that forced a 6 foot 4 inch (190 centimeter) semiprofessional football player to exercise his chest in the same way as a 5 foot (150 cm) day car teacher was not likely to provide anything in the way of an exercise program that looked as though it had been individually tailored, nor were the results likely to suit such disparate individuals with jobs and pastimes that make widely different physical demands. And since neither of our exercisers was the "average" person for whom nearly all exercise machines have been designed, both of them probably ended up with an injury or two. (This is not to say that there is no place for such machines in an exercise program, or for certain exercises, only that they need to be used sparingly, and with discretion.)

Second, many of the people who used gyms and attended exercise classes regularly began to develop just those chronic injuries that the researchers said could be avoided by following a more specifically designed exercise program.

And third, typical of international demographic trends, the customers at health clubs were becoming older and more demanding in terms of what was being offered. Step and aerobic programs seem

When starting a new exercise program, beginners can have one-on-one training.

A good diet should be part of any health regime.

balancing effort made to train and adapt the mind to match the new, improved muscle function. And so the start of a mind–body approach to what goes on in the gym began to take hold.

There is now a whole new emphasis on being healthy rather than just fit. This implies much more of a holistic approach to the whole person, and there is now an increase in the demand for one-on-one training by personal trainers. The trainers themselves have acquired a broader range of skills, and have moved beyond the rigorous, army-style instructors of a few years ago, embracing "lifestyle coaching" and nutritional advice, as well as coaching for specific leisure activities, such as golf or skiing. The result is a much better-educated exerciser making much bigger demands on his or her health club or gym.

Fortunately, those responsible for scheduling class timetables did not have far to look to find a ready-made, functional exercise program. One of the basic tenets of Pilates is that strong movement emanates from a strong base, and so it quickly gained space in health clubs and popularity with customers, especially as it

less appropriate forms of exercise for those of advancing years, especially as great care is required to avoid overuse injuries if you attend such classes frequently.

These three factors, together with a big increase in media coverage of health and fitness issues, changed the approach to exercise. As a result, designers of exercise programs started to consider more functional exercises that prepared the exerciser for his or her real life. It became clear that just exercising the muscles is a waste of time if there is no

For many of us, walking to and from work is the only exercise we get.

and for the new exerciser coming from a sedentary background. Those three categories, especially the last one, probably account for the bulk of the population, which might explain the continuing, and growing, popularity of Pilates exercises.

Very few people today have physically active jobs, and most of us enjoy relatively

had been designed by its founder to take account of just those chronic injuries to the back and elsewhere that figured so largely in the new research. At the same time, it is very adaptable to the specific circumstances of individuals. Pilates exercise programs have been developed for both pre- and post-natal women, for example, for older people,

A half-hour walk twice a week makes a difference.

sedentary lifestyles. Doing the weekly shopping and carrying it from the car is just about the biggest physical effort we may make unless we have a yard, and then we may only move a lawnmower around the lawn and do a bit of weeding. Housework, too, is now largely a question of pushing relatively lightweight electrical appliances around the home or pressing buttons; there is little to tax the muscles. Yet all of these activities are frequently cited as being a major cause of the injuries that give rise to chronic pain.

Compare this to the lives of our grandparents and great-grandparents. For their generations, work was largely physical:

many men worked on the land or in factories, and women performed virtually all of the tasks in the house, many of which were physically demanding, certainly in comparison to the housework of today. People also walked greater distances, simply because automobiles were far less common and a bicycle or the bus were often the only alternatives.

Eating habits were once dictated by price and the limited range and quantity of food supplies. With the advent of refrigeration and cheap air-freighting, our diets are no longer governed by what is in season. We enjoy a far wider range of foods than our immediate ancestors, and can choose

Almost all fruit and vegetables can be bought all year round nowadays.

pretty much whatever we like rather than having to make do with seasonal, local produce. Food manufacturing has also ensured that meals come ready-prepared, with a minimum of effort needed by the consumer to set them on the table. The downside is that much of our diet is over-refined, oversalted, and oversweetened.

Given a general population with a sedentary lifestyle, exercising infrequently and eating little in the way of fresh food, it is hardly surprising that heart disease and other ailments generated by deficient cardiovascular systems have increased dramatically.

Although people generally live longer than before, many have a lower quality of life because they are plagued by diseases associated with obesity. So for those who wish to avoid this fate, the health club has become the first port of call. Initially, this often proved a disappointing experience, which is one reason why there is such a high attrition rate for gym membership. But as they began to understand their own needs better, customers started, and continued, to make very specific demands in terms of classes and equipment.

Many of us have very sedentary jobs.

Health Problems Caused by a Sedentary Lifestyle

These are some of the more common and obvious problems that today's sedentary lifestyle causes.

- Adult-onset diabetes. A disease largely associated with obesity and hence with poor diet and lack of exercise.
- Back pain. Back pain clearly has many causes, but is worse in those who are overweight and in those doing little or no cardiovascular exercise.
- Decreased brain function. A large number of studies have shown that the supposed loss of brain function that occurs as we age can be prevented and, in some cases, reversed by doing cardiovascular exercise.
- Strokes. Many studies have shown results similar to those suggested for brain function (outlined above).
- Heart disease. Cardiovascular exercise and a healthy diet are critical factors in reducing the risk of heart disease.
- Osteoporosis. While this disease is largely a result of hormonal and genetic influences, there is growing evidence to show that the increase of the disease among men results from the reduction in the amount of load-bearing exercise that they do. A resistance-exercise program may alleviate some of these problems.
- Chronic pain in the knees, shoulders, and neck may be a sign of osteoarthritis. Evidence now suggests that movement and gentle exercise can help to delay the onset of these symptoms, and that continued exercise after the symptoms have appeared can help to reduce the pain.
- Various cancers. We are becoming increasingly aware of the influence of environmental effects that can precipitate cancer in those who may be genetically prone to specific types. Diet and exercise habits loom large among these environmental influences.

Although depression is not directly attributable to either a sedentary lifestyle or diet, an exercise regime is an effective way to tackle the problem, and some studies have shown it to be at least as effective as drug therapy. Many of these problems can be eliminated or reduced by improving cardiovascular function through exercise and healthy eating.

Posture

As more evidence emerges about the circumstances that influence our well-being and overall physical and psychological health, it becomes clear that how we spend our everyday lives is of enormous importance. We all spend a great deal of our time sitting: in automobiles, in front of computers, and on sofas that are too low and often too big. This affects the way that we stand and sit, so that our shoulders hunch and round forward, the curve in the upper (thoracic) part of the spine increases, and the lower (lumbar) part of the spine also tends to round.

In biomechanical terms, this sets us up to suffer an injury the moment we do decide to do something physical. If you need evidence of this, just ask your doctor how many cases of back or shoulder pain he or she sees immediately after the first fine, warm weekend of spring. Such weather encourages us to tend to the yard, to play baseball with the children, or to go off on a bike ride. After a winter of doing nothing, our backs need gentle exercise to regain their fitness, and injury is common in these circumstances. So maybe our grandmothers were right when they made such a fuss about how we sat

It is easy to get into the habit of adopting a bad posture.

at the table and told us not to slouch as we walked around.

The ideal posture has been defined as "a position in which muscle and skeleton are balanced in such a way that, regardless of the position from which the two systems are working or resting, the supporting structures of the body are protected from injury or progressive deformity. This position will provide the optimum conditions for muscles and joints to work at maximum efficiency."

This definition is one way of saying that if we were to stand and sit in good positions in the first place, it would be relatively easy for us to move in ways that would not hurt us, and that would keep our backs, in particular, free of pain and injury.

How, then, should we stand and sit? It is here that some of the more recent research about injury (usually injury to athletes) can be of assistance to us all in our everyday lives. In a very general way,

Starting a new form of exercise should be taken slowly if you are to avoid injury.

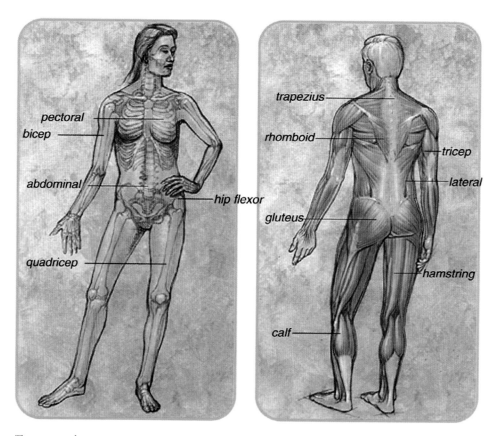

pectoral
bicep
abdominal
hip flexor
quadricep

trapezius
rhomboid
tricep
lateral
gluteus
hamstring
calf

The core muscles.

the research indicates that provided that individuals have "core musculature" that works well, they are much better able to deal with situations that have the potential to cause injury. And when they are injured, they also have the ability to recover more quickly.

So our problem is now reduced to a more manageable question. We know that strong, active core muscles protect us in situations that might cause injury. If we can identify those muscles, we then need to make them strong by exercising them. Experimentally, the core muscles have been categorized as the deep abdominal muscles; the muscles responsible for rotation at the waist; some muscles in the lower back; and, more controversially, the gluteus muscle in the buttocks.

Crucially, all of these muscles are involved in the maintenance of good posture, as well as providing stability through the center of our bodies. But, critically, these muscles are inhibited from working in those circumstances when we provide ourselves with something for our backs to lean on when we are seated, and when we choose, inevitably, to stand in a poor position.

For a large proportion of the population, these muscles therefore function poorly, if at all. This results in individuals with bad posture, leading to inefficient movement and a central support system (core) that doesn't work very well.

So far, I have been delivering just the bad side of the story. There is definitely a good side. We know that a strong core protects us, and we now understand how to make the core strong.

Pilates has been around for nearly one hundred years, and its founder could have known little about the specific function of what we now call the "core." However, his intuitive and pragmatic understanding, that without a strong center, exercising the extremities is somewhat pointless, has put

his exercise method at the forefront of the changes in the way that fitness and health are now being achieved.

We need a strong core. Pilates exercises, as well as some of the newer forms of core-strengthening exercise regimes, such as Swiss-ball training, can achieve this for us.

We need a healthy cardiovascular system. A properly planned and executed cardio-exercise program that avoids too much repetition and consequent overuse injuries, and that also includes a logically consistent stretching program will, over time, deliver this, provided that no prior lasting damage to either part of the system has already been caused.

We should eat five servings of fruit or vegetables a day.

idealistic proposal can certainly become a practical reality. Essentially, the approach that I have adopted for clients has been structured with Pilates exercises as the central part of the solution. These are then coupled with core and cardiovascular exercises, stretching, a sensible diet (with supplements if necessary), and time spent on more soothing activities.

What I have not suggested here is any particular mind–body combination. From my own experience, I know that some people are happiest in meditative mode, and that

We need a sensible and healthy way of eating that delivers all of the necessary vitamins and minerals, as well as the range of fats, proteins, and carbohydrates that we need in order to maintain our bodies and protect them against damage in an increasingly hostile environment.

Finally, we need to remove excess stress from our lives so that we are in a position to allow the other three factors to work for us. Hobbies, pastimes, pets, meditation, and sports are all ways of achieving this. The solution is highly individual, and not one that could, or should, be prescribed by anyone else.

I do not claim that any of this is an original solution to our problems, but this somewhat

Meditation can play a role in any fitness regime.

An active lifestyle is a positive one, both mentally and physically.

exercise is a real chore for them. Equally, because I work in an exercise environment, I have come across many individuals for whom the most relaxing activity is a physical workout of such intensity that the rest of us would need to lie down for a week to recover from it. For these individuals, ten minutes spent sitting still and reading the newspaper is about as much as they can take! People are very different from one another, and we therefore need to focus on the individual when looking for solutions, addressing not only their reported symptoms and specific issues, but looking at the whole person so that each individual is able to take responsibility for his or her own well-being.

What, and Who, Is Pilates?

Joseph Pilates was born in Düsseldorf, Germany, in 1880. As a child, he was sickly, suffering from, among other things, rickets (usually a disease associated with poverty and a poor diet) and rheumatic fever (which may damage the heart). Undaunted by such a poor physical start in life, he determined to make himself as fit and healthy as possible.

He started by looking around and studying the kind of exercises that people with physically demanding careers (like gymnasts) were already doing, and practiced these for himself, succeeding well enough so that in adolescence he was used as a model for a textbook of anatomy. More importantly from our point of view, he became proficient in a number of sporting disciplines, such as skiing and diving. He also spent time training as an acrobat. His taste and range—in exercise, at least—was wide, and he also looked at the philosophies of the East and the exercise practices that Eastern philosophers had advocated when he was developing a regime for himself. The emphasis on breathing and some of the floor exercises are ample evidence of these influences.

In 1914, Pilates was in London, England, employed in teaching the police force his self-defense techniques. As a German citizen, he was interned at the outbreak of World War I. He was sent to a camp on the Isle of Man, where he worked as a hospital nurse and orderly, and his belief in exercise was such that he soon had the other internees practicing versions of his regime. The influenza epidemic that killed millions worldwide five years later spared his fellow internees. He and others ascribed this to the efficacy of his exercise method and the rigor with which it had been applied. Any suggestion that this might have had something to do with the relative isolation of the Isle of Man, and of the camp, seems to have been dismissed.

After the war, he returned to work in Germany, still training policemen, but this time in Hamburg. During the interwar years, Germany was seething with ideas and inventiveness, both politically and in the world of the arts, and there is some evidence that it was then that Pilates first came across dancers and their particular exercise problems. However, Pilates disliked the increasingly militaristic political environment and left for the United States in 1926. On board his ship, he met a young woman, a nurse named Clara, who later became his wife.

Once established In New York, he opened a studio at 939 Eighth Avenue. By the 1940s, he was well known among the dance community, and by the 1960s, actors and athletes had joined the likes of George Balanchine and Martha Graham as regular attendees at his studio.

What Does the Pilates Exercise System Do For You?

Given Pilates' early life experience, it is not surprising that at the heart of his approach to living is the idea that you need a body that will never let you down if you are to be able to live a healthy, happy life. Most of us would agree with him wholeheartedly. However, he takes the whole concept farther, arguing that the flexibility and fluidity of childhood movement is something that we have no reason to lose as we age.

Pilates believed that the less flexible, more tentative adult is produced by an accretion of inappropriate postural and movement habits. If we are serious about our health, we can lose these habits (or at

least the majority of them) by taking control. By this, he meant having our muscles behave in a way that we consciously decide on rather than in a way that has been developed by careless habit.

Here, Pilates was very much in tune with modern ways of thinking. What he said was that we must each take responsibility for our own health, and that we must develop an attitude of strength and confidence in relation to our bodies so that we can be in charge. In some ways, this makes embarking on a Pilates course easier, since the values of self-reliance and self-help are common currency in a world in which healthcare costs are soaring and treatment-rationing has become prevalent. What we need to ensure, though, is that we keep these ideas of being self-reliant and in control conscious rather than unconscious in our exercise sessions. It is vital that the element of being in control of our bodies is in the forefront of our minds while we perform the program.

For those who can do this, and who take the exercise program seriously, the following benefits are possible.

Pilates Is Open to All, Regardless of Age or Physical Ability

Pilates is accessible to everybody, however fit or unfit. It may be of benefit to the young or the elderly, and to people of every age in between, and you do not have to be a physical person to perform the exercises. Of course, those people who were good at sports at school may be quicker at learning the exercises than the rest of us, but anyone can do them.

No Impact

The exercises do not involve impact (by which I mean that no running or jumping is involved), so those with injured joints can participate relatively safely.

If you are a new exerciser, if you are on medication, or if you have an injury or any chronic condition, you should consult your doctor before starting any exercise program, including Pilates, however.

Exercise Without Stress, Strain, or Pain

If properly carried out, the exercises involve no stress, strain, or pain. This is a huge advantage to those starting a new program since it allows you to exercise every day and very slowly to build your fitness. This contrasts with most other kinds of programs that state that your muscles may be painful or stiff for a couple of days after the session, especially when you first start. New exercisers understandably often take the view that if it hurts it cannot be doing them any good, and quickly abandon the effort.

Strengthening the Core

The whole purpose of the exercises is to strengthen those muscles of the core, which, when they are sufficiently developed, allow us to make properly controlled movements of the limbs. This limits the risk of injury, both in everyday life and in more active leisure pursuits.

Strength and Control

What Pilates exercises give you, once you have begun to master them, is strength with control. This advantage may to some extent repeat the point made above, but it bears

repeating. Individuals who undertake strength programs in the gym frequently become injured. This mostly happens because the strength that they develop runs far in advance of their control of movement; the technique fails, and injury is the result.

Balance and Stability

Logically, if you add the above benefits together, others accrue as a consequence. If you become skilled at moving and using muscles only with full control, improvements in balance and stability will also become apparent. Undeniably, this is one of the major benefits that older participants discover. Older people are more prone to falls, which often result from having muscles that are underused, and joints that are stiff, painful, and inflexible. Older bones break more easily and heal a great deal less

efficiently, and rehabilitation can be a long and expensive process. The Pilates system is an excellent method of reducing this particular vulnerability.

Postural Alignment

As the muscles become more balanced and controlled, posture improves. Rounded shoulders straighten, spines lengthen and have curves in the right places, necks become longer, and heads that are pushed forward, in front of the chest, gradually pull back to be more in line with the body. This results in less general "achiness" and joint discomfort, and can reduce the incidence of headaches. As the chest is opened up, lung function improves. Joseph Pilates' emphasis and insistence on lateral breathing is an aid to this, and asthmatics often find the techniques of great benefit.

Bodies Look Lean, Not Bulky

Once all of these muscular and postural changes have occurred, the esthetic benefit that is so widely claimed for Pilates as a system begins to emerge. The long silhouette so much admired by our body-conscious fashion industry and society at large results from having balanced and stretched muscles under full control.

However, if the only reason why you take up Pilates is with the objective of achieving the silhouette of a model like Naomi Campbell or Elle McPherson, you may be doomed to disappointment. Even Pilates cannot change basic biological material. If you are short and square to start with, you will end up being short and square. You will almost certainly look less short and less square, and therefore leaner and less bulky, because you will be more balanced, but your basic body shape will remain the same.

Mind–Body Communication

Finally (and this claim is made for many exercise disciplines, but is an important by-product of the Pilates process), you should develop a mind and body that are more in tune. This is not a claim for any mystical process, but a Pilates program forces you to think about your body and what you are asking it to do, so you tend to listen to your body and use your brain more in everyday life. The benefits of this, in my view, are at least twofold. A brain that listens to the body that it controls becomes a much better manager, so less fatigue, greater efficiency, and fewer injuries should result.

The Eight Principles of Pilates

It seems to be a characteristic of human beings that they look for structure in everything. If they don't find it, they impose it. Joseph Pilates structured his exercise programs by adopting a set of what he called "principles," to which all of his exercises, and the people who performed them, had to adhere.

The Eight Principles of Pilates

So we have got to the stage where we are ready to begin to look at the exercises that Pilates developed. As with any exercise program, it is important to prepare properly. In this case, because Pilates lays such emphasis on the involvement of our brains in the exercise process, it is very important to understand what he thought of as the underlying principles — philosophy, almost — of what the method entails.

When you first come across a Pilates exercise program, your impression may be that it is a fairly hit-and-miss collection of exercises and practices from a number of other disciplines. Elements of yoga are blended with bits of the Alexander technique, while sophisticated moves from the world of gymnastics follow easily recognizable, everyday gymnasium activities. And if this is what you see, that is largely because that's how Pilates developed his own personal program. He researched many individual disciplines, practiced most of them, and selected the exercises and processes that he believed contributed the most to the development of his own strength, enabling him to overcome what he saw as his childhood weaknesses. He used these exercises for himself first, and as he became confident of their value, filtered them through to his pupils. If he found anything that didn't work for him, he discarded it, and continued to refine the process as his experience as a teacher expanded.

While Pilates is not exactly unique in the way that it is organized under a number of guiding principles that may sound familiar, as a package, these principles begin to define the philosophy of Pilates—both the man and the exercises—in a very specific way. When this is understood, and the student is able to accept that each and every principle is equally important, and that no part is optional, then the principles become a very powerful guide to how to make the program really work.

Adherence to the eight principles is a major part of performing the program.

These are: concentration, control, center, breath, fluidity, precision, routine, and isolation.

Pilates was, in many ways, a man of action rather than a man of theory. As a result, it can be difficult both to explain and understand these principles. Words do not easily convey physical principles. Nonetheless, because they are so important in enabling the correct performance of Pilates exercises, it is important to spend some time trying to comprehend what they mean. If you succeed in understanding the exercises before you start them, then the time taken to reach your potential will be accordingly reduced.

Concentration

Given that Pilates thought that any exercise performed with an unengaged brain was no exercise at all, it is hardly surprising that the principle of concentration is regarded as the heart of the Pilates philosophy. The muscles do not run on automatic in Pilates—the mind and brain need to be engaged and focused the whole time. Concentration joins the mind and body, which then cooperate to perform the various movements and to exclude anything extraneous to them. Without concentration, the Pilates method does not really exist. Pilates movements may seem simple before you try them, but are generally very challenging. Only by using concentration are we able to employ some muscles in stabilizing in preparation for movement, and then to focus on producing the movement accurately. In practical terms, this means that when you are performing your routine, you need to be sure that you are as relaxed as you can be, in surroundings that are as undistracting as possible, and with enough time to make you certain that you will not be interrupted.

Control

For Pilates, control meant very much what it means in everyday language: brain control and muscle control. The brain tells the muscles what movement to perform, at what intensity and to what extent, and the muscles respond by doing just that: moving at just the right intensity and to the correct extent, neither more nor less. This particular principle is the one that people are most likely to fix on when they first start a Pilates program, and it can be particularly difficult at first. What we are trying to achieve are relaxed, flowing movements, nothing jerky or forced, and this can only be attained through concentration and control at the minutest level.

No one is likely to get this right from the start. Many movement skills, especially those that require coordination, are learned in a process of trial and error: learning to walk necessitates falling down. This learning process is helped enormously by imagining what it looks and feels like to get it right. Sports psychologists, among others, call this process "visualization." Don't be worried about making mistakes—it's one of the most important ways to learn.

Center

Pilates sometimes referred to what I have been calling the "core" or the "center," as "the body's powerhouse." What he meant by this was that the center of the body is the location from which all movement is generated (provided that the body is functioning properly). He was in some ways extraordinarily prescient and knowledgeable in this, as modern research shows that his intuition, instinct, and experience were uncannily accurate.

At this center, we have a large number of muscles: those of the abdomen and lumbar spine, as well as of the hips and buttocks. These muscles, as is normally the case in nature, have more than one function. At the most obvious level, they support and protect the soft organs of the abdomen. As we begin to understand more about the structure and biomechanics of our bodies, this function increasingly appears to be secondary to the function of supporting and protecting the lumbar spine. Most exercise practitioners now refer to this area as the "core," and it is   .

The "core" muscles protect the spine from damage during any form of movement.

becoming increasingly obvious that an active and strong core is a prerequisite if movement at the extremities (the arms, legs, head, and neck) is not to damage the spine or the joints of the limbs. In this context, the fact that *Homo sapiens* was not, according to evolutionists, originally designed to function in an erect stance is important. Without a strong central core, humans could never have moved from the horizontal to the vertical.

Joseph Pilates enunciated this principle more than fifty years ago. His point was that the process can be viewed like ripples in a pond: the disturbance (movement) begins at the center of the pond and emanates outward, to the edges (the limbs). Contrast this with other forms of exercise regimes in which the focus is on the extremities: push, pull, punch, kick, jump, run, swing, and so on. If you start at the center, however, the lengthening and stretching that are the essentials of muscular activity can occur while the spine is being prepared and protected at the same time. Try to think of the core muscles as the conductors of a muscular orchestra that keep time and control the rhythm and strength of the movements of the other muscles.

Breath

Breathing and breath control are at the heart of the Pilates exercises. As a teacher, I have found that students often find this one of the harder aspects of the technique to master. The principle is relatively easy, but the performance is more difficult to achieve. Controlling the breathing rhythm at the same time as developing a new breathing technique can make this principle a pretty daunting one.

Pilates was concerned that most people tend to breathe with the upper part of their chests, or even hold their breath during certain phases of exercise. At the very best, this can inhibit the precision of the movements required, and in many cases it makes it impossible to complete the movement accurately.

Breathing in this way is inefficient and uses perhaps a quarter of the lungs' potential: the volume of air that is exchanged through the lungs like this is relatively small, maybe as little as one-quarter of the possible total. The amount of oxygen delivered to the circulatory system is consequently much reduced, as is the

Abdominal breathing is a key aspect of Pilates.

amount of carbon dioxide that is expelled from the body.

A breathing method that completely inflates the lungs with new air would clearly be more efficient and beneficial. And a mechanism for doing this exists and is often employed by singers, musicians, and actors, people who need to control their breathing in their professions.

Lateral breathing, which Pilates taught and is still advocated, is similar to these controlled techniques. Instead of lifting the ribcage to inhale, focus on the muscles of the abdomen and the lower ribcage and try to expand them outward. The main muscle for respiration—the diaphragm—then begins to work as it should. By pushing down into the abdomen, it creates a partial vacuum around the lungs, and air from outside is drawn downward, to the bottom of the lungs, expanding them fully. The outward effect of this is that the ribs expand laterally, to the sides (this movement gives the technique its name), and with air delivered right to the bottom of the lungs, the efficiency of oxygen delivery and carbon-dioxide removal is enormously improved. Breathing becomes more controlled and less forced, with no need to snatch a breath. This more relaxed approach allows us to coordinate the breath with the exercise, to establish a rhythm.

Fluidity

"Fluidity" was the word that Pilates used to describe the flowing movements used to perform his exercises. This fluidity extends from the repetition of each individual exercise to the transition from one exercise to the next: the exercises and all of the repetitions form part of one continuous whole. There are no rests between exercises and repetitions, and transitions should be seamless. There should be no feeling of haste, nor of time moving slowly. Movements should be the same in terms of intensity, distance moved, and the speed with which they are carried out. In many ways, this is a "feeling" concept.

As you perform the exercises of your program and become both more adept and more familiar with it, you will begin to feel that it is somehow taking on a life of its own, a rhythm that feels absolutely right. This is a different experience for each person, and relates to the

individual's coordination of limbs, joints, muscles, and tendons. When you reach this point, it can feel a bit like a runner's high. This principle is the hardest of all to demonstrate to a class of many people as the instructor is more likely to be explaining the technique, which distracts students from feeling the fluidity.

Precision

If you watch Pilates practitioners as they exercise, you'll see that one of the most notable features of the movements is that each repetition is exactly the same. This kind of exactness in execution is essential, and critical to making the whole process effective. Moving with precision is bound to be a difficult task for a new student who is trying to perform unaccustomed muscular movements and new breathing techniques, while listening to instructions and working out at the same time. This particular principle may therefore be the one that we are most inclined to let slip, and discussing the habit of precision with people who are not used to it can be very difficult.

Dancers of this caliber encapsulate all of the principles, but precision perhaps most of all.

Many athletes, dancers, and acrobats who use their bodies to perform spend their working lives trying to perfect just such a habit. A Pilates routine without precision is compromised, and its exercise value reduced. Practice, coupled with patience and the expenditure of sufficient time on the early stages of learning the routines will be amply rewarded in terms of the extra benefit that the exercises will deliver. If you are as haphazard as I, the precision thereby acquired may well carry over into other areas of your life, so there may be unexpected benefits, too.

In practical terms, mastering this particular principle will require a lot of your time and concentration. The most useful tools are a strong sense of how to visualize each movement of the exercise and a mirror to help you to check your progress.

Routine

The principle of routine is similar to the idea of rehearsing for a performance or performing the repetitions of most exercise routines. It is a very basic way in which muscles learn. It establishes recognition of,

and familiarity with, the exercises, so that when we come to each movement in the routine, neither the brain nor muscles are required to work the whole thing out. Familiarity lubricates the process. As long as we apply focus and concentration, by establishing the routines, we will improve the way that we execute the exercises and will enhance the skills that we bring to the process.

Isolation

The difference between the way that Pilates thought of isolation and the way that most exercisers regard it is that for Pilates, isolation is only the initial part of the exercise, and, in many respects, a relatively minor part at that. Most exercisers concentrate on isolating a particular pair of muscles—biceps, for example—and then exercising them to exhaustion. Pilates used isolation as a first step to integration. All of the exercises require focus and concentration on a complex, coordinated movement. But each movement is made up of several individual muscles cooperating to achieve a focused, concentrated, and coherent whole movement. Given that everyone is a different shape, attaining the necessary skills for this new exercise program will require different degrees of effort, and different ways of isolating in order to achieve the balanced body that the Pilates technique will build for us.

A Set of Clues

None of the above is meant to put you off. The eight principles are harder to understand in print than they are in performance, and should be seen as a helpful set of clues rather than a rigid set of rules. As you master a few of the basics, what appears difficult on the page will become much more easy to understand. The principles are simply an organized statement of what is required to perform any exercise program effectively.

All athletes, gymnasts, tennis players, or football players use the principles of control, focus (concentration), fluidity, precision, routine, and isolation to effect integration. Breath and centering may be less obvious, but weight lifters, swimmers, and yoga practitioners would also subscribe to these concepts, even if they use, and think about, them in slightly different ways.

Preparation

Most of us have had the experience of organizing, straightening up, and cleaning our homes. Those who take little pleasure in it will have learned that the task is made easier through proper preparation. The same is true of an exercise program: if you get ready properly, the "chore" element is reduced to a minimum.

Preparation

If what you have seen and read so far has convinced you that Pilates may have something to offer you, then there are a number of ways to prepare yourself for an exercise program. These are the very basic techniques and positions with which you will need to become familiar in order to master the program.

These preliminaries are necessary precursors to the exercises, and an early mastery of them will help to ensure that you are able to perform the program with minimum risk of injury.

As a first step, making an effort to improve your posture when standing and sitting will help to make you much more conscious of your body and of how it moves and functions. Since good posture requires control and activation of the core muscles, this will increase your awareness of these muscles and will enable you to locate and use them much more easily when you start the program.

The "core" comprises a number of muscles, the most important in Pilates being the transversus abdominis and the various gluteus muscles, along with the muscles that comprise the obliques. In reality, though, it is all of the muscles of the abdomen, lower back, hips, and buttocks. When they are correctly coordinated, these muscles, along with the diaphragm, fix the center of the body and enable us to use our arms and legs independently, without having to move the arms as a counterbalance to the legs.

Pilates called this the "center" or "powerhouse," and its overriding importance is that it allows precise and accurate movement with minimum risk to the structures of the spine. From this, it follows that the proper functioning of the core is a prerequisite to good posture. So if we make a start by aiming for good posture, the spin-off should be an introduction to how to engage the structures of the core. It is important to emphasize that everyone develops their own technique for making the core work for them, so it may take a while for other people's explanations to make sense to you. Do not give up: it doesn't take long for it to all click, and you will recognize it the minute that it does.

Most of us do not stand or sit well. The tendency is to exaggerate the natural curves of our spine, which are designed to minimize the effect of physical shock on our systems by flattening them or rounding them farther. The normal spine has three curves: the lower-back or lumbar curve; the upper-back or thoracic curve; and the cervical or neck curve. These are designed to dampen and dissipate the shock waves that pass through our bodies as a result of our feet thumping onto the ground every time that we take a step.

Any distortion to these curves results in an extra shock running through the various joints of the body. Shock and damage to the sensitive areas around the head (caused by boxing, for example) may also result in swelling of the brain tissues. Additionally, the structures of the spine, the intervertebral disks, and the vertebrae themselves will eventually be damaged if the spine's natural curves are chronically distorted.

It is obviously worth spending some time and effort reasserting the usual curves in your spine and making the necessary adjustments to your posture to achieve this.

Alignment Sequence

1. Stand with the feet parallel and a hip-width apart. ("Hip-width" means that the center of the knees, ankles, and feet should all be in a vertical line, level with the pelvic bones in your hips.)

Good posture.   Bad posture.

2. Now try to ensure that weight is evenly distributed between the toes and heel of each foot. Softening the knees very slightly will help. Imagine that each foot is a rectangle, and that the weight is supported equally along the four sides.

3. From this position, you can now lengthen the spine upward, toward the ceiling. I always do this by thinking about lifting my chest as high as possible. Normally, this will feel as though you are stretching out the abdomen and pulling up through the upper back because most of us stand or sit in a slumped pose.

4. Next, the shoulders need to be as wide as possible. Those who lead quite sedentary lives tend to have shoulders that round forward in both the horizontal and vertical planes, meaning that the weight of the arms and anything that they are carrying hangs from the muscles of the neck. This leads to neck pain. Try to achieve a good position by rounding the shoulders forward as far as possible and then pulling the shoulder blades back together as far as possible. Somewhere between the two positions you will feel tension come off the neck. For most people,

this usually means that the hands are hanging loosely just before and outside the thighs.

5. Finally, attend to the head and neck by lengthening the neck toward the ceiling. I imagine trying to add an inch to my height by pushing my skull as high as possible while keeping my chin pulled in. Be very conscious of the chin: don't allow it to lift or your head to tip back.

Seated Posture

1. Once seated, position your feet a hip-width apart.

2. The knees should be directly above the feet.

3. Repeat steps 3 to 5 of the previous procedure to align and stretch the spine.

An open chest and normal spinal curve mean that lungs and limbs can function properly.

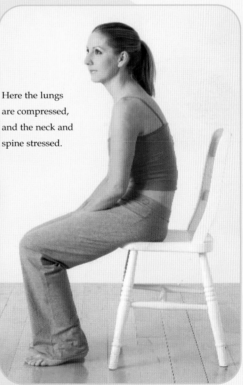

Here the lungs are compressed, and the neck and spine stressed.

There is a bit more to sitting well than may at first appear. Ideally, when you are seated, the knobby bit of bone that sticks out at the top of your thigh (the x process) should be higher than the knobby bit of bone that sticks out at the outside of your knee (the y process). This allows you to sit so that your back is long and your chest is high. If you are seated with your knees higher than your hips (which is common when sitting in an armchair or sofa), you have to round your lower spine to be able to manage it. In the long run, this can be quite damaging.

Having established "best practice" for getting to the starting point of a Pilates routine, there are a number of techniques and some terminology to clarify before moving on to the exercises themselves.

Neutral Spine and Neck

This is a phrase that Pilates teachers use to indicate that the spine (usually the lumbar spine) should have a neutral or natural curve in it while you are performing the exercise. This is the same as the curve that you generate when you correct your posture as described above.

Similarly, the term "neck in neutral" means keeping the neck in exactly the same position that you found for it in the posture exercise above. And in teaching instructions, it is usually a phrase designed to encourage you not to let your head drop or tilt back.

You can practice both of these positions by lying on a mat. Many Pilates exercises are performed lying on your back (supine),

Wrong position.

so that finding the right position and practicing other techniques while lying in this way is both important and helpful.

Lie on your back, hands by your sides and legs extended. Feel the curve that your lower back makes in relation to the floor. Then bend your knees and bring your feet toward your buttocks. As you do this, you will probably feel the curve change. Continue until your feet are as close in as you can manage, and note the curve in relation to the floor. From here, there are two ways to proceed. Use the one that suits you best.

1. Gently slide your feet away until they have traveled roughly half of the distance from one of the extremes to the other. You should feel that the curve that we talked about is now also roughly halfway between the two extremes. This is neutral spine for you.

Finding neutral.

Correct neutral spine.

2. If this doesn't work for you, start from the fully extended leg position and just move your feet back through the range until you reach the most comfortable position. This, too, is neutral spine.

If neither of these gets you to the position in which you think you should be, then you can be more mechanical about the whole thing and lie on the floor with your feet as close to you as you can comfortably get them. Round your spine as much as you can, then reverse and flatten it as much as you can. Do this a couple of times, and again choose somewhere between the two extremes where your spine feels most comfortable and "strong." This is neutral spine.

At this stage, neutral neck is about comfort and nothing else. When you are lying on your back with your spine in neutral, you need to lie with your torso as long as possible and your head in such a position that your face is parallel with the ceiling. For many, if not most, of us, this will be uncomfortable because the top vertebra of the spine and lowest vertebra of the neck protrude to a greater or lesser extent. If this is the case, use a rolled or folded towel to support your head; as your posture improves, the problem should ease. (See the postural exercises at the end of the book.)

Abdominal Muscles

Not everybody finds it easy to make the lower abdominal muscles, with which the Pilates exercises are mainly concerned, work. It is worth practicing consciously switching them on and off before starting a full program.

The most important of the muscles is the transversus abdominis (T.V.A.). I find that most people can activate it if they are in a prone position. Even if they find it very hard to get the muscles to work, they understand, and have a feel for, exactly what is required.

1. Adopt a kneeling position on all fours, with the knees directly beneath the hips, and the hands directly beneath the shoulders. Ensure that the spine is in neutral. Next, let your abdominal area hang as low as possible, while still maintaining a neutral spine and neck. Then breathe into the space that you have just made, using lateral breathing.

2. Pull your navel up, toward your spine, so that the abdomen moves and the spine stays stationary. Hold the position, then relax the abdominals as you breathe out. Repeat the process.

1.

2.

Do about a dozen repetitions, and then gently get to your feet and stand in a position of good posture, as described earlier. Repeat the exercise, but this time in the vertical position. If you have difficulty accessing the muscles while you are upright, keep practicing while kneeling, and gradually you will be able to move to the vertical position.

Breathing

Breathing control causes new students the most problems. This does not mean that we do not know how to breathe, although many of us do breathe very badly, but that it is something that we do so unconsciously that it can be very difficult consciously to control. Stress is just one of the factors that contributes to shallow breathing using the muscles of the neck and upper ribcage.

Shallow, quick breaths are insufficient for sustained and controlled muscular effort, and lungs that fill with oxygen-rich air on every inhalation and expel large quantities of carbon dioxide with each exhalation are a great deal more efficient. Pilates' method of lateral breathing uses the diaphragm and lower-chest cavity and is similar to the type of breathing required of singers, actors, and athletes.

As you breathe out, you pull your diaphragm up, into your ribcage, and your lower ribs contract inward; as you breathe in, the diaphragm pushes down, into the abdomen, and the lower ribcage expands outward, to the side. The rhythm is slow and deliberate; each breath is full.

If you find this difficult, try a number of other techniques. Lie on your back, with your head and neck in neutral. Place a heavy object, like a book, on your navel. Focus on this when you breathe: as you breathe in, it should lift, and as you breathe out, it should fall. Then focus on the rise and fall of the book while paying attention to the movement of the lower ribcage, and try to make it expand as you inhale and contract as you exhale. Once you have managed this, get to your feet and place your hands on the outside of your lower ribcage, with your elbows sticking out, to the sides. As you inhale and exhale, focus on the points of your elbows: with each exhalation, they sink down and in, and with each inhalation, they lift and move away from your sides.

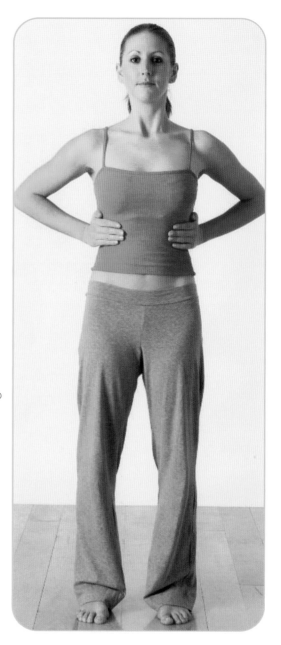

Breathing in.

Breathing out.

This takes a little while to perfect, but do not panic about it. You will eventually find that it comes quite naturally.

When you first start a program, you may find it difficult to concentrate on activating the abdominals, holding neutral spine, and keeping the movements that you are making controlled. Then, on top of all of this, you are going to ask your brain and body to take conscious control of your breathing, so that you inhale and exhale in a different way, and in a controlled rhythm that coincides with the movements that you are making. Not surprisingly, many students find this difficult, and the whole thing

consequently quickly falls apart, which is often extremely disheartening.

Concentrate on the core and neutral spine first. Do your best to make the movement, and as your control of the core and spine gradually become more instinctive, focus on making the movement precise and controlled.

Finally, without undervaluing the importance of breath control, I suggest that you breathe normally at first and practice lateral breathing when you can. Then gradually add the correct breathing technique for the rhythm right at the very end. Doing this usually makes the process far more manageable.

Balancing Exercise for the Nervous System

Finally, it is always a good idea to prepare the nervous system for a new exercise program, particularly if your body is not used to much in the way of physical activity. Waking up the nervous system so that the brain and muscles can begin to harmonize is one way of minimizing the risk of injury (already very small in the case of Pilates exercises) and for preparing the body to learn the new skills that we expect of it as quickly and efficiently as possible.

I use balancing exercises for this purpose, which may seem strange if you have already seen Pilates exercises, most of which are performed lying or sitting on the floor. However, muscles, nerves, and senses become fired up when we test the balance systems of the body (because such a huge degree of coordination is required to perform the exercises), preparing them all for use, and training them to respond more accurately and efficiently when we make new demands of them.

There are any number of balancing exercises available, but I usually use either of the following two approaches.

First, stand on a hard surface in bare feet, if you can. Stand properly, in a good posture. Keep the spine long and with neutral curves, the head high, the shoulders wide, and the knees soft.

With one foot planted firmly on the floor, raise the knee of the other leg so that just

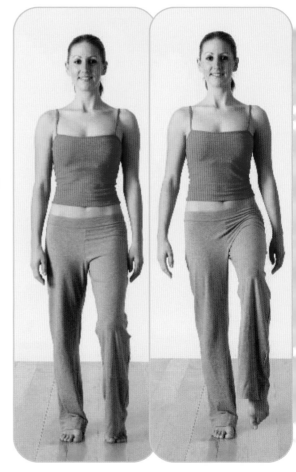

your toes are touching the floor. When you feel confident, raise the knee about 6 inches (15 cm) higher, so that you are balanced on one leg. Focusing on lifting the knee and on keeping upright, look away into the distance. Hold for a count of 15 and then change to the other leg. Repeat both sides a couple more times. You could even try the exercise with your eyes closed, although make sure that you have something to hold onto as this can be surprisingly difficult at first.

Alternatively, if you have a Swiss exercise ball, try this exercise.

Seat yourself on the ball, facing a mirror, if you can. Make sure that your knees and feet are a hip-width apart, and your feet are directly beneath your knees.

Breathe in, and pull your navel in tight. Then lift your right hand above your head and left knee about 4 inches (10 cm) vertically. Hold for a count of 15. Change sides. Repeat half a dozen times on each side.

Preparatory Checklist

By doing the preparation outlined above, you have made yourself ready to begin a Pilates program. Before setting off, however, go through this checklist to ensure that all is in order and that you have the right equipment.

1. Check with your doctor that the exercise program will not be harmful to your health. This is especially important if you haven't exercised for a while, if you have a preexisting injury (see below), if you are on medication of any kind, or if you are pregnant. Pregnant women should note that it is inadvisable to start a new regime: some of the exercises are dangerous if performed during pregnancy, so consult a good teacher before even considering taking up Pilates.

2. If you already have an injury, make sure that you continue any remedial stretches and exercises that you have been doing. Do not let these drop until your doctor, trainer, or physical therapist says that you can.

3. You will need enough space to accommodate a mat and Swiss exercise ball (if you are going to use one). Remember that some exercises require you to spread your arms out wide and to roll from side to side.

4. Make sure that the room temperature is comfortable. We are all different. You know if you prefer a cooler atmosphere than other people do, or if you tend to feel chilly and like the heat to be turned up. Take account of this when selecting your exercise space.

5. Do not try to hurry your program. Remember that you need to stretch, warm up, and cool down. You should not rush, so tailor your program to the time that you have

available. Focus and quality are crucial to a successful Pilates program: it is better to perform a short, good-quality program than a long, haphazard one.

6. You will need an exercise mat. Do not try to cut corners and do without one. Spines and backs may be generally robust, but you will be trying to support your weight along your spine or on your elbows and knees. The last thing you want is for the discomfort of a hard surface to interfere with the quality of your program.

7. You will need something with which to support your head. This could be a foam block, a folded towel, or a pillow that ensures that you can comfortably rest your head and neck in neutral. Again, do not take shortcuts here. Knowing that you are comfortably and precisely in neutral makes it easier to perform the exercises.

8. Make sure that you wear appropriate clothing. You need to be able to move on the floor, stand up, lie down, and possibly use an exercise ball. Gym clothes are fine if you feel comfortable in them, otherwise stick to loose (not baggy) trousers and a top. You do not need shoes or socks.

9. Try to ensure that you have a space with the right atmosphere in which to work out. You need to be totally focused on what you are doing, so turn off the phone and T.V. If you like to listen to music, make it mood music. Make sure that the rest of your household knows that interruptions will not be welcome.

Most of this advice is common sense, but all of the above points are about how to achieve the focus required to perform Pilates exercises. In addition, there is another important point.

The mat and ball exercises described in this book are not easy, but none of them generates impact, and, if they are being performed correctly, they do not overstress the muscular tissues. The small progressions that you are asked to make should only be tackled once you are confident that you are strong enough to perform them. In this way, no damage to muscular tissue or joints can be caused, and you should not feel any soreness afterward, although you may be aware that you have worked hard. Muscle soreness can be generated in a number of ways. It may result from poor (or no) stretching, from excess lactate left in the muscles after exercise, or from minute tearing of the fibers that make up the muscle if they are overloaded during exercise. This soreness is a sign of inefficient exercise behavior as far as the Pilates student is concerned, because it means that the body's resources are diverted to controlling the inflammation and repairing the damage. If you feel sore after a Pilates program, the chances are that you have been overdoing it a bit, so pull back a little and exercise more slowly next time.

Injury

Barring accidents, you are extremely unlikely to injure yourself while performing the exercises described here, even if you do not get the techniques quite right. Nonetheless, care and caution are always required.

Many people with existing injuries, especially injuries to the foot, knee, back, or neck are advised to go to Pilates classes to help remedy their conditions and to alleviate pain. A Pilates program can be most helpful for individuals with chronic pain or a chronic or recurring injury, but such a program should probably not be the first step. Acute injuries need acute remedies: if you start a Pilates program with a sore back, it is almost guaranteed to become more sore. Initial treatment for such injuries needs to be individually tailored and more hands-on than will ever occur in a class.

In addition, your medical practitioner should ensure that you are through the treatment stage and ready for rehabilitation before you join a general Pilates class.

That is not to say that you should not perform Pilates at all in these circumstances, but if you do, you should seek out a teacher who will teach you on a one-on-one basis and who has some specialized knowledge of the kind of rehabilitation that your specific injury may require.

Stretching and Warming Up

There has been a reasonable amount of controversy regarding the value of stretching before a workout. However, there is certainly no evidence that it is harmful to the body, and warming up is definitely beneficial, so do not be tempted to skip this chapter.

Stretching and Warming Up

Stretching and warming up before your Pilates workout is just as important as for any other exercise routine. However, you can combine the two to save a bit of time, and provided that you have performed them correctly, it will ensure that all of the muscles and joints that you are going to use are ready and able to be tested.

The warm-up gently increases the blood flow to the muscles by raising your heart rate and encouraging blood to move to the skin's surface in order to help you to keep your body temperature under control. Gentle walking on the spot and some knee lifts will do this. Add some lateral (side-) stepping and some arm lifts to the side, front, and over your head, continue for about five minutes, and you should then be ready to stretch. But remember that if you are cold because of the room temperature, you will need to extend the warm-up period until you feel warm.

When you stretch, it is important to stretch all of your muscles. Even if you find that you do not feel some of the stretches, still perform them, but don't hold them and move on to stretches for the next muscle group. Try to ensure that all of your muscles are properly stretched to prevent injury, however. Concentrate especially on any muscles that feel tight as they need preparation to enable them to operate through a full range of movements. I have developed a stretching routine starting from the floor and then working upward to mobilize my joints and stretch my muscles.

Toe Wave

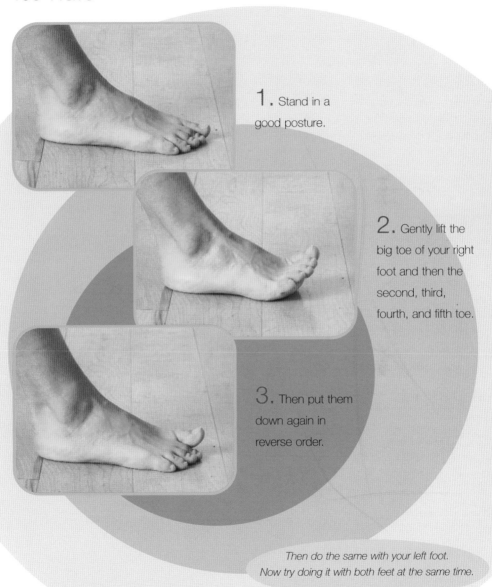

1. Stand in a good posture.

2. Gently lift the big toe of your right foot and then the second, third, fourth, and fifth toe.

3. Then put them down again in reverse order.

Then do the same with your left foot.
Now try doing it with both feet at the same time.

Foot-arch Activation

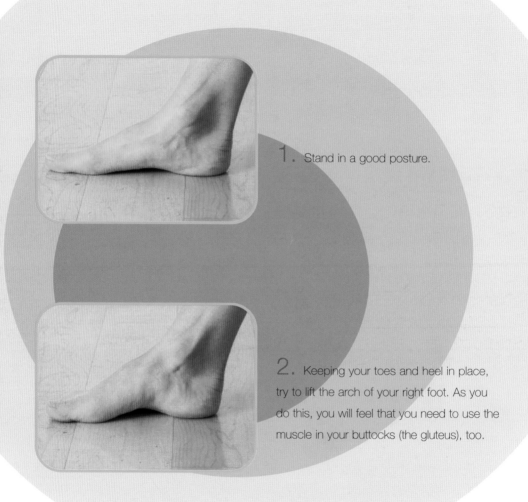

1. Stand in a good posture.

2. Keeping your toes and heel in place, try to lift the arch of your right foot. As you do this, you will feel that you need to use the muscle in your buttocks (the gluteus), too.

Repeat with your left foot.

Ankle Mobilization

1. Stand in a good posture.

2. Lift one foot off the floor while balancing on the other. Use something to support you if you feel too unstable.

3. Move the ankle of the raised foot in as many different directions as you are able.

4. Make sure that you reverse any rotating movements.

Change feet and repeat.

Tiptoe Stand

1. Stand in a good posture.

2. Without throwing your weight, gently try to use your feet and legs to lift you up, onto your toes. Hold for a count of five, then lower.

Repeat two or three times.

Calf Stretch

1. Position your feet in a split stance, with both feet facing forward.

Hold for ten seconds and then change legs. Repeat twice more.

2. Keep your body straight from your back heel to your shoulder, then lean forward (imagine that you are as straight as a plank of wood). Keep your back heel on the floor and feel the stretch in the calf of your back leg.

Hamstrings *(Back of Thighs)*

1. Stand in a good posture. Step forward with one leg.

2. Keep your front leg straight and bend the knee of your back leg, keeping your weight on your back leg.

3. Holding your spine in neutral, lean forward from your hips until you feel the stretch in the back of your front thigh. Hold for five to ten seconds, then change legs.

Repeat twice more.

Quadriceps/Hip Flexors *(Front of Thighs)*

1. Kneel on the mat. With one knee on the mat, position the foot of the other leg so that the bend of that knee is just over 90 degrees.

2. Push your hips forward very slightly, thereby reducing this angle, and then tuck your hips underneath you.

3. Feel the stretch in the front of the thigh of your rear leg.

Hold for five to ten seconds and then repeat twice more.

Gluteus *(Buttock Muscles)*

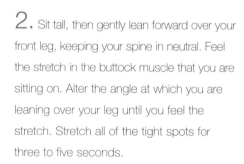

1. Sit on your mat and arrange your legs as shown in the photograph, so that all of your joints form 90-degree angles.

2. Sit tall, then gently lean forward over your front leg, keeping your spine in neutral. Feel the stretch in the buttock muscle that you are sitting on. Alter the angle at which you are leaning over your leg until you feel the stretch. Stretch all of the tight spots for three to five seconds.

Change legs and repeat.
Repeat twice more for each leg.

Back and Abdominals

Be very careful with this stretch if
you suffer from back pain.

1. Stand tall, keeping
your hands by your
sides. Bend your knees,
breathing out at the
same time.

2. As you breathe in,
straighten your knees
and extend your arms
above your head while
stretching your back as
much as you can.

Repeat three or four times.

Back and Waist

1. Sit cross-legged on the mat with your spine in neutral. Stretch one arm as high as you can toward the ceiling.

2. Then grasp your raised wrist with your other hand.

3. Keeping both "sitting bones" on the floor, gently pull yourself into a stretch with the hand that is holding the wrist. Hold for ten seconds.

Change sides.
Repeat three or four times for each side.

Chest and Shoulders

1. Stand adjacent to a doorway or corner of a wall. Bend one arm and lift your elbow to shoulder level. Now rest your entire arm against the wall.

2. Gently turn your torso away from the wall. Feel the stretch in your chest and the front of your shoulder. Hold for ten seconds.

Change sides.
Repeat three or four times for each side.

Shoulder Rolls

1. Stand in a good posture.

2. Using your shoulder muscles only, and not the muscles of your neck, roll your shoulders forward for three to five rolls.

3. Then roll them backward for three to five rolls.

Neck and Shoulder Stretch

1. Stand in a good posture.

2. Keeping it in the same plane the whole time, tilt your head to the left as far as you can, pushing your right shoulder down as much as possible.

3. Then gently rest the weight of your left hand on the right side of your head. Hold for ten seconds.

Change to the opposite side and repeat.

Roll-down

This exercise warms up the back and loosens the spine in flexion. It is often used as part of the press-up exercise, but I prefer to use it separately before the exercise session proper because it provides an early warning for those with back pain as to whether they will experience discomfort, thereby enabling them to take special care when performing those exercises that put the back at risk.

1. Stand in a good posture. Breathe in and pull your navel in tightly.

2. Bring your chin to your chest, letting your head and hands hang heavy.

Remember that this is not an old-style
attempt to touch your toes,
but an attempt to curve your back
as much as possible.

3. Slowly round your spine from top to
bottom so that your hands are gently
lowered to the floor. Keep your knees soft
and try to keep your bottom still. Breathe
out slowly as you descend.

4. At the bottom of the stretch, breathe in
again and then reverse the curling of the
spine, moving from the bottom to the top.

*Repeat the whole up-and-down
movement three or four times.*

The Exercises

There is now some debate as to how many mat exercises make up the Pilates repertoire. Those given here are adaptations in some cases, but all Pilates teachers would recognize them.

The Exercises

These programs are really only suggestions for the exercises that you may need or want to perform as you progress with your Pilates workout in terms of your strength and skill. They are not prescriptive, in the sense that you must master one level before progressing to another (although, in many instances, it is best to be sure that you can perform the easier exercise before moving on). Even if you are a more advanced student, you may sometimes want to include certain beginners' exercises in your program, even if only to check that you still remember how and what to do. Or you may be feeling fatigued or may have had a long period when you were unable to practice as much as you would wish.

Some of the exercises will often be ones that you find either particularly easy or particularly difficult. Do not feel that this should be a limiting factor. Mix and match from the programs as you feel able.

Similarly, the order of the exercises is deliberately flexible. When I was first taught and started teaching Pilates, I believed that you could design a single program order that would work for everybody. Experience has taught me differently, however. In order to experience a smooth flow and feeling of fluidity when moving from exercise to exercise, it is very important that each individual follows a program that suits him or her rather than a "one-size-fits-all" program.

So as you become familiar with the exercises, experiment with the order and with making the transition from one to the next. Gradually, you will find that certain ways of ordering the program feel comfortable, while others feel less so. Stick with the comfortable ones and then refine them until what you are doing seems absolutely right to you. Equally, you may not—indeed, you probably should not—want to perform every exercise at every session, so you may need to devise two or three programs from the range of exercises provided within all three levels.

Above all, try to take the opportunity to relax and enjoy the exercise process. Exercise professionals like me tend to take what we do very seriously and often inadvertently pass on that seriousness to students without making it clear that the whole process of exercising should be fun, too. If you make it enjoyable for yourself, you are much more likely to be regular and thorough in the performance of your program, and thus gain maximum benefit from it.

Beginners

Push-up

1. Kneel on all fours on the mat, with your spine and neck in neutral. Your hands should be level with your shoulders, but slightly outside them. Align your knees directly below your hips. Breathe in and pull your navel in tightly.

2. Resist the move as you make it, and press your chest to the mat, keeping your neck in neutral. At the bottom of the move, breathe out and push your chest away from the mat. Resist the move again.

Repeat five to ten times.

Swimming *(Lying Down)*

1. Lie on your front with your arms and legs extended. Your arms should make a 45-degree angle with your torso, and your thumbs should be turned upward to point toward the ceiling. Breathe in and pull your navel in tight.

2. Slowly stretch your right arm and left leg away from your torso. As you stretch your arm, your leg will lift easily. Try not to let your leg lift more than your arm (your back may feel the pressure if you do), and as your arm and shoulder lift, let your head (your neck should still be in neutral) lift with them.

Breathe out and lower.
Repeat for the other side. Repeat 10 times on each side.

The One Hundred

1. Lie on your back on your mat, with your neck and spine in neutral and your arms by your sides. If necessary, support your head with a folded towel and keep your neck in neutral.

2. Round your spine into the mat, then lift first one leg, then the other, to a position in which your knees are above your hips and your shins are parallel with the floor. Relax your spine to neutral again, breathe in, and pull your navel in tightly.

Hold the position for a count of one hundred, breathing in for five beats and out for five beats.

Maintain the neutral position of your spine and neck at all times. If you feel that you cannot, rest for a while and then start again. At the end, gently lower your feet to the floor.

Repeat three times.

Plank

1. Lie on the mat with your elbows directly below your shoulders, and your forearms resting flat on the floor. Breathe in and pull your navel in tightly.

2. Keeping your spine and neck in neutral and your knees on the floor, lift your hips so that they reach an imaginary line running between your shoulder and knee. Keep your shoulders relaxed and your stomach tight. Continue to breathe. Hold for a count of ten, then gently lower your hips back into the starting position.

Repeat three to five times.

Rolling Back

1. Sit on the mat with your feet on the floor, your knees bent, and your back in neutral. Place your hands, facing forward, on the floor beside you, and relax your elbows and shoulders. Breathe in and pull your navel in tightly.

2. Tilt your pelvis under and gently roll back, onto your shoulder blades. Breathe out and, keeping your stomach tight, roll back up again. As soon as you are strong enough to remove your arms from the mat, move on to performing the exercise with your arms holding onto your legs.

3. Try to keep your legs in one position as you roll as this makes the abdominals do the work rather than using the weight of your legs as a counterbalance.

Perform ten repetitions.

Single-leg Stretch

1. Lie on your back on the mat, with your neck and spine in neutral.

2. Push your spine into the mat and gently raise one leg, then the other, so that your knees are directly above your hips, with your shins parallel to the floor. Relax your spine to neutral and breathe in, pulling your navel in tightly.

3. Gently push your right knee away from you, keeping the left one completely still. Breathe out and bring your right knee back.

Breathe in and repeat for the left knee. At first, you can simply extend your leg at a slight angle to the vertical, but as you become stronger, move the angle to about 45 degrees. Keep your lower back and pelvis absolutely still during the exercise.

Repeat ten times for each side.

Roll-down/Roll-up

1. Sit tall on your mat, with your knees bent and your feet on the floor. Breathe in and pull your navel in tightly.

2. Curl your pelvis underneath you so that your back rounds, and then continue to round your spine back down, toward the mat, keeping your feet on the floor. As soon as you feel that your feet want to lift themselves off the floor, or that you cannot keep your navel pulled in, use your abdominals to pull your back up into the starting, sitting position.

As you become stronger and more experienced, you will be able to roll back farther, until your shoulder blades touch the floor. Do not go any farther than this, however.

The next step is to lie flat on your back on the mat, with your arms and legs extended.

1. Breathe in, pull your navel in tightly, and then slowly bring your arms (still fully extended) past your shoulders. Using your abdominals, lift yourself up into a sitting position.

2. Reach all of the way forward to your toes, breathe again, and roll back down, onto the mat. On the way back, keep your arms low, and make sure that the movement is slow and controlled. Breathe out gently as you roll.

Repeat five to ten times.

Side Kick

1. Lie on your side, with your legs held long, but not overextended. Make sure that your hips are stacked vertically, one on top of the other, that your spine is in neutral, and that your head is resting on your lower arm. Your upper hand should be resting on the mat, in front of your navel, to help you to balance.

2. Breathe in and pull your navel in tightly. Slightly lift both legs, breathe out, and hold.

3. Breathe in, pull your navel in tightly again, and lift your top leg so that it is level with your hip.

4. Then, breathing out, push your leg forward, but only as far as you can while maintaining your balance and the alignment of your neck and spine. Breathe in and repeat the kick. Try to increase your range as you perform the repetitions.

Perform ten repetitions for each side. When you are stronger, progress to keeping your upper arm stretched along your body so that it is not assisting your balance.

Single-leg Circle

1. Lie on the mat, with your spine in neutral, knees bent, and feet on the floor. Breathe in and pull your navel in tightly.

2. Lift your right leg so that the knee is directly above your hip and your lower leg is parallel with the floor.

3. Breathe out, then breathe in and pull your navel in tightly again. As you breathe out, draw five clockwise circles with your knee, keeping your hips, pelvis, and spine absolutely stationary.

4. Breathe in again, and as you breathe out, draw five circles with your knee, this time moving in the opposite direction. Think of the hip socket as the pivot from which the movement is being generated.

Remember to keep your circles even and gradually to make them a little bigger. Perform up to ten circles, two or three times in each direction, with each leg.

Single-leg Kick

1. Stretch out face down on your mat. Bring your elbows directly beneath your shoulders, with your forearms flat on the mat, and chest slightly lifted.

2. Breathe in and pull your navel in tightly, while keeping your spine in neutral and your thighs in contact with the floor. Bend one knee so that the foot points at the ceiling.

3. Breathe out, kick your foot toward your bottom, bring your leg back to the vertical, and then kick again. Breathe in and lower your leg to the floor.

Repeat for the other leg.
Perform a total of five to ten for each leg.
Remember to keep your navel pulled in tightly throughout.

Shoulder Bridge

1. Lie on your back, your spine and neck in neutral, knees bent, and feet on the floor.

2. Breathe in, pull your navel in tightly, then tilt your pelvis toward the ceiling and lift your hips while uncurling your spine from the mat and breathing out.

3. When you regain the neutral-spine position, you have lifted your hips high enough. Breathe again and move your hands in a semicircle so that they are resting behind your head on the floor.

4. Breathe out and bring your hands back beside your hips. Breathe in again as you hold the position, keeping your hips parallel with the floor. Then, breathing out, gently lower your hips to the floor by rounding your spinal vertebrae back onto the mat.

Repeat ten times.

Side Bend

1. Sit on one side with your elbow resting on the floor and your forearm pointing forward. Your ankles, knees, and hips should all be in a single line, and your other arm should be resting in front of you. Your upper body should be aligned, and your neck and spine should be in neutral.

2. Breathe in, pull your navel in tightly, and move your weight onto your elbow and knee. Breathing out, lift your hips.

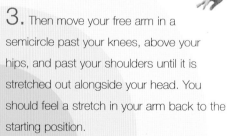

3. Then move your free arm in a semicircle past your knees, above your hips, and past your shoulders until it is stretched out alongside your head. You should feel a stretch in your arm back to the starting position.

Perform five to ten repetitions for each side.

Mermaid

1. Lie face down on the floor, with your forehead resting on your hands, your heels together, toes turned out, and legs held long. Breathe in and pull your navel in tightly.

2. Squeezing the muscles in your bottom and the back of your thighs, lift the full length of your legs off the floor. Make sure that you keep your head on your hands and focus on your legs. Try not to use your back.

Perform two sets of ten.

Intermediate Program

The division of exercises into programs is, to some extent, arbitrary. If you find something too hard or too easy, experiment with a substitution, and if you find something that works better, stick with it.

Intermediate Program

Changing from the beginner's program to the intermediate program is not a single-step process. I think of the exercises in a program as individual organisms that mature at different times. Once you have adopted this concept, you will realize that you still find some of the beginner's exercises hard, while others are relatively easy to perform.

This is the time when you should begin to think of changing your program. Do not change from the beginner's to the intermediate program all at once, however, but keep the beginner's exercises that you still find hard or challenging in your new program, at the same time gradually substituting the harder versions of exercises that are not challenging enough from the intermediate program. In this way, you should be able to achieve a fairly smooth transition with no strain.

Half Press-up

1. Get on your hands and knees on the mat. Make sure that your hands are set slightly wider than a shoulder's-width apart. Make a bridge between your hands and knees, holding your spine and neck in neutral and making your back as long as you can. Breathe in and pull your navel in tightly.

2. Press your chest to the floor and breathe out as you push yourself back to the starting position. Keep your navel pulled in throughout.

Repeat for two sets of six and then gradually work up to two sets of ten.

Swimming *(Kneeling)*

This exercise strengthens the shoulders and the muscles in the back of the legs.

1. Kneel on all fours on your mat, with your knees directly in line with your hips. Your thighbones should be vertical, and your hands directly beneath your shoulders, with your spine and neck in neutral. Breathe in and pull your navel in tightly.

2. Gently stretch out your right arm and left leg as far as you can without tilting or rotating your hips or shoulders. Your leg should never rise above your hip, and your extended arm should be level with your shoulder. Your torso should remain parallel to the floor at all times.

Breathe out, lower, and repeat for the other side.
Repeat ten times for each side.

One Hundred Full

1. Lie on your back, with your spine and neck in neutral, knees bent, and feet on the floor. Breathe in and pull your navel in tightly. Push your spine against the mat.

2. Lift one knee so that it rises vertically above your hip. Return your spine to neutral.

3. Pull your navel in tightly and raise your other leg to the same position. Keep your toes pointed. Hold this position until you can no longer maintain your spine.

4. Raise both arms so that your hands are just above your hips. Then breathe in for a count of five and out for a count of five.

Hold for a total of ten in-and-out breaths, and repeat three times.

Roll-up

This helps to control strength and flexibility.

1. Lie on the mat on your back, with your arms and legs extended and spine and neck in neutral.

2. Breathe in and pull your navel in tightly. Bring your arms over your head while keeping your navel pulled in tightly.

3. Using your lower abdominals, round your spine up, off the mat, and breathe out slowly as you reach toward your feet.

4. Breathe in again and gently round your spine back down, onto the mat.

When you are moving (in both directions), think of it as lifting and lowering one vertebra at a time.

Single-leg Stretch

This exercise improves strength and control.

1. Lie on your back, with your spine and neck in neutral, knees bent, and feet on the floor. Breathe in and pull your navel in tightly. Raise your knees to a position in which they are vertically above your hips and your shins are parallel to the floor.

2. Keeping one leg absolutely still, push the other away until it makes a roughly 20-degree angle to the horizontal. Breathe out and gently lift your head and shoulders off the floor, maintaining a neutral spine.

Lower your head and shoulders. Breathing in, slowly bring your leg back to the starting position and repeat for the other side. Perform ten repetitions for each leg.

The Seal

This exercise helps your mobility.

1. Sit tall at the front of your mat and balance on your sitting bones, with your feet apart and holding onto your ankles. Breathe in and pull your navel in tightly.

2. Now gently roll back, onto your shoulder blades.

3. Then, while breathing out, use your abdominal muscles to roll back up into the balanced starting position.

4. Pull yourself up tall so that your spine comes into neutral again, and hold the balance for three beats by "clapping" with your ankles three times.

Repeat ten times.

The Crab

This exercise is good for improving core strength and spine mobility.

1. Sit tall at the front of your mat and balance on your sitting bones, with your ankles crossed and holding onto them. Breathe in and pull your navel in tightly.

2. Keeping your heels close to your thighs, gently round your spine and roll back onto the mat as far as your shoulder blades.

3. Breathe out as you roll back up into the balance position, still keeping your heels close to your thighs. Stretch your spine into neutral again, keeping your feet off the mat.

Repeat five to ten times.

Double-leg Stretch

1. Lie on your back on the mat, with your head, neck, and spine in neutral. Push your spine against the floor while gently raising one leg so that the knee is vertically above your hip and the shin is parallel to the floor. Do the same with the other leg. Put your feet together. Relax your spine into neutral again and keep your shoulders relaxed.

2. Breathe in and pull your navel in tightly. Gently push your knees away from you so that your legs are extended. Only extend them as far as you can while holding your spine and pelvis absolutely still, or until you feel that the strain on your back is too great. If you wish, you can extend your arms in a circle, out and back. Take them to an angle of about 45 degrees to your torso and to the floor.

Breathe out, and bring your arms back in a circle past your shoulders as you pull your knees back toward your hips until your hands touch your knees again. Repeat five times with your arms circling in one direction, and five more times with your arms circling the opposite way.

One-leg Circles

An exercise for improving core strength and hip mobility.

1. Lie on your back on the mat, with your arms by your sides, legs extended, and your head, neck, and spine in neutral. Breathe in and pull your navel in tightly.

2. While maintaining neutral, slowly lift one leg so that your toes point toward the ceiling. (If you need to, allow your knee to bend to achieve this position.)

3. Using your hip as an axis, rotate your leg in a clockwise direction, keeping your pelvis still.

4. Circle your leg ten times clockwise, then reverse the direction and rotate your leg counterclockwise.

Holding your spine in neutral, slowly lower your leg to the floor. Repeat for the other leg.

Spine Stretch

This stretch improves the mobility of the spine and hips.

1. Sit tall, with your spine in neutral and your legs stretched out in front of you. Place your feet as far apart as is comfortable. Your legs should ideally be relaxed, but not bent at the knee. However, many people have tight hamstrings, and if you are one of them, bend your knees so that you are able to hold your spine in neutral.

2. Gently extend your arms and place your hands between your legs. Breathe in and pull your navel in tightly.

3. Round your spine forward from your pelvis to your neck, slightly tilting your pelvis "through" your hips as you breathe out and stretch your spine, with your arms moving toward your feet. Breathe in again, and at the full extent of the stretch, hold it gently. Then return to the starting position while breathing out.

Repeat ten times.

Shoulder Bridge

An exercise for improving core strength and spine mobility.

1. Lie on your back on the mat, with your neck, head, and spine in neutral, knees bent, and feet on the floor, about a hip-width apart.

2. Breathe in, pull your navel in tightly, and tilt your pelvis toward the ceiling. Breathing out, slowly lift your spine off the mat, vertebra by vertebra, until it makes a straight line between your hips and your shoulders.

3. Breathe in and move your hands in an arc over your head until they rest on the floor.

4. Hold your hands there, and while slowly breathing out, roll your spine back down, onto the mat. Bring your hands back into the starting position.

Repeat ten times.

Side Kick Kneeling

An exercise to increase core strength.

1. Kneel on the mat, with your spine held in a good posture.

2. Extend one leg sideways along the floor, making sure that your foot and the knee of your other leg are in alignment with your torso.

3. Gently lean away from your extended leg until the fingers of your opposite hand just touch the floor, again keeping everything aligned. Breathe in and pull your navel in tightly.

4. Lift the foot of your extended leg off the floor and touch your temple with your free hand.

Repeat five to ten times for each side.

5. Breathe out and slowly push your free leg forward from the hip. Extend it as far as you can while maintaining your balance, and do not allow your hip to roll. Breathe in and return to an aligned position, then breathe out as you repeat the movement.

Side Bend

This will improve core and stabilizer strength.

1. Sit on one side, with your lower leg extended and the knee of your upper leg bent. Cross your upper leg in front of the lower one. Place the hand of your lower arm flat on the floor, directly beneath your shoulder. Breathe in and pull your navel in tightly.

2. Push down on your top foot and hand to lift yourself to make a bridge between these two points. Make sure that your spine is aligned and in neutral, and that your hips are vertically in line.

3. Breathe out and arc your top arm in line with your body so that it circles to finish in line with, and above, your head. Feel the stretch, then breathe in again and retrace both arm and hip movements back to the starting position.

Repeat five to ten times for this side, and then do the same for the other.

Leg Pull-up

This complex movement strengthens the core, arms, and shoulders, and stretches the chest and abdominals.

1. Sit on the mat, with your legs extended in front of you, your spine and neck in neutral, and your torso leaning back slightly and supported on your hands, which should point forward. Breathe in and pull your navel in tightly.

2. Lift your hips toward the ceiling.

3. Keeping your stomach tight, breathe out and lift one fully extended leg as high as you can while maintaining neutral and keeping your hips parallel to the floor.

Repeat five to ten times for each leg.

Breathe in, lower your leg, and change to the other. While lifting your leg, you may find it helpful to focus on the heel as this seems to help to activate the appropriate muscles for the job.

Teaser

This exercise improves core strength.

1. Lie on your back on the mat, with your head, neck, and spine in neutral. Push your spine against the floor while gently raising one leg so that the knee is vertically above your hip and the shin is parallel to the floor. Do the same with the other leg. Put your feet together.

2. Extend your arms above your head,

3. Breathe in, pull your navel in tightly, and then extend your legs at an angle of roughly 45 degrees.

4. Hold this position as you breathe out and move your arms in an arc until they are parallel to your legs.

Repeat five to ten times. Then breathe in and lower your arms back into the starting position and breathe out as you lower your legs onto the mat.

5. Slowly curl your torso up off the mat, vertebra by vertebra, to make a "V"-shape with your legs. Breathe in and lower your torso back onto the mat, trying to control the movement with your core.

Hip-twist Preparation

An exercise for core strength and control
with hip mobility.

1. Sit on the mat in a neutral posture,
with your knees bent and toes on the floor.

2. With your arms spread wide and
positioned slightly behind you, lean back a
little to rest on your fingertips. Breathe in,
pull your navel in tightly, and twist your legs
to one side so that your knees fall
to that side.

3. Breathe out, and, balancing on your
sitting bones extend your legs from this
angle. Breathe in and bend your knees
again. Twist to the other side and breathe
out while extending your legs once more.

Repeat five to ten times for each side.

Scissors

This exercise challenges the core while strengthening the legs and hips.

1. Lie on the mat on your back, your spine in neutral, your knees bent, and your hands by your sides.

2. Now extend your legs until your knees make an angle of about 120 degrees.

3. Breathe in and pull your navel in tightly. Then, keeping your hips and pelvis still while breathing out, raise one leg, maintaining the knee's 120-degree angle.

4. At the top, hold, and breathe in. Then, while breathing out, lower your leg again, stopping just before your foot touches the mat. Repeat for the other leg.

Repeat the whole exercise five to ten times for each leg.

Swan Dive

This exercise strengthens and coordinates the muscles of the legs and core.

1. Lie on your stomach, your hands just outside your shoulders, your legs extended, heels together, and toes turned out. Make your back as long as you can.

2. Breathe in and pull your navel in tightly. Lift your chest and shoulders off the mat, keeping your hips on the floor and your head and neck in neutral the whole time. Exhale, and lower your trunk back onto the mat.

3. Breathe in again and then, squeezing your buttocks and breathing out, lift the entire length of your legs off the mat as far as you can.

4. Breathe in again and lower your legs back onto the mat.

Repeat five to ten times.

Jackknife

An exercise to improve spine flexibility and core strength.

1. Lie on your back, with your legs extended, arms by your sides, and neck and spine in neutral. Breathe in and pull your navel in tightly.

2. Squeeze your buttocks and thighs while breathing out, then, using your abdominals, lift your legs until they are pointing directly at the ceiling.

3. Breathe in again and continue the movement of your legs through your spine, so that you lift your torso off the mat, starting with the lowest vertebra and rounding your spine, until you are resting on your shoulders and arms.

4. Breathe in again and then gently reverse the process, controlling your torso to round it back down onto the mat.

Saw

This exercise stretches the obliques, thighs, and spine.

1. Sit on your mat, with your spine straight and in neutral, and your arms extended to the sides and level with your shoulders. Extend your legs in front of you, with your feet flexed and held about 24 inches (61 cm) apart.

2. Breathe in, and as you breathe out, slowly turn to one side from your waist. Everything below your waist should stay still, and your arms should move with your shoulders.

3. Reach across and down with one arm and hold the outside of the opposite foot.

Breathe in again as you lift your torso and rotate back to the starting position. Then breathe out as you turn in the opposite direction and repeat. Repeat five to ten times for each side.

Side Kick

1. Lie on your side on the mat, with your legs and lower arm extended. Make sure that your hips are stacked vertically, one on top of the other. Your top hand should be resting on the floor in front of your navel for balance, and your head should be resting on your lower arm.

2. Breathe in, pull your navel in tightly, and lift your legs so that the top leg is level with your hip.

3. Then exhale and push your top leg forward as far as you can while still maintaining your balance and not allowing your hip to move at all.

Breathe in as you bring your leg back. Breathe out and repeat, gradually making the movement bigger as you grow more confident and have stronger control of the core. Repeat ten times, then roll over onto your other side and repeat.

Rocker Open Legs *(Preparation)*

This exercise tests core strength while the limbs are moving.

1. Sit tall on your mat, with your spine and neck in neutral, feet on the floor, and knees bent. Grasp your ankles with your hands.

2. Then lean back, taking your feet off the mat. Find your balance position. Breathe in and pull your navel in tightly. Extend your legs so that you are sitting in a "V" shape.

Breathe out and lower your legs toward the floor, but hold the balanced position. Breathe in again and repeat. Repeat ten times in total.

(Full Version)

1. When you can perform the preparation exercise confidently, move on to the full version. To perform this, repeat the first part of the preparation sequence so that you are sitting in a "V"-shape, then breathe in, tuck your pelvis underneath you, and gently roll your spine back onto the mat.

2. When your shoulder blades touch the mat, breathe out and roll back up, using your abdominals to control the movement.

Repeat ten times in total.

Single-leg Kick

An exercise to strengthen the chest, arms, and backs of the thighs while stretching the quads and abdominals.

1. Lie face down on a mat, with your legs extended, your elbows directly beneath your shoulders, and your forearms on the mat. Breathe in and pull your navel in tightly.

2. Lift your hips toward the ceiling, bridging the weight between your knees and elbows.

3. Breathe out, and, pointing your toes, raise and extend one leg to its full length.

4. Breathe in and kick your heel toward your bottom. Breathe out, extend your leg again, and lower it to the mat.

Repeat ten times for each side.

Double-leg Kick

This exercise stretches the back, shoulders, and quads, and strengthens the gluteus and hamstrings.

1. Lie on your mat on your stomach. With your palms facing the ceiling, move your hands to the small of your back.

2. Breathe in, pull your navel in tightly, and stretch your legs away from you as you lift them slightly off the floor.

Breathe out and lower your feet to the floor. Repeat ten times for each side.

3. Breathe out, and, from this position, kick both heels back, toward your bottom, three times.

Advanced Program

The introductory note for the previous chapter applies twice as much here. Experiment and adjust the exercises, seeking advice where you need to, so that the program that you develop and follow is unique to you.

Advanced Program

As with the transition from the beginner's to the intermediate program, the change from the intermediate to the advanced is a gradual transition, not a sudden switch. It requires active consideration of all of the program exercises on your part, and for each you need to decide whether you are performing it easily, with difficulty, or not quite correctly.

Do not be in too much of a hurry. Your body will tell you when you have made a mistake by increasing the level of difficulty too soon. If this happens, simply revert to the previous level of difficulty for that exercise and wait until you have developed sufficient strength and skill to make the transition with some strain, but no pain. If in doubt, you can always stick with the easier option until you have the opportunity to consult a teacher. Most Pilates teachers are happy to give advice and guidance.

One Hundred *(Full Version)*

1. Lie on your back, with your spine and neck in neutral, knees bent, and feet on the floor. Breathe in and pull your navel in tightly. Push your spine against the mat.

2. Lift your knees so that they rise vertically above your hips, and then return your spine to neutral. Pull your navel toward your spine again and slowly extend your knees to the point at which you can just maintain your spine in neutral.

Breathe in for a count of five and out for a count of five; hold for a total of ten breaths in and out and then repeat three times.

Roll-up

An exercise for control, strength, and flexibility.

1. Lie on the mat on your back, with your arms and legs extended, and spine and neck in neutral.

2. Breathe in and pull your navel in tightly. Bring your arms back over your head, keeping your navel pulled in tightly.

3. Using your lower abdominals, round your spine up, off the mat. Breathe out slowly as you reach toward your feet.

4. Breathe in again and gently round your spine back down, onto the mat.

To help you to perform this movement, try to visualize lifting or lowering one vertebra at a time.

Rollover

This exercise improves spinal flexibility and strengthens the abs and arms.

1. Lie on your back, with your legs extended and arms by your sides, at an angle of 30 degrees to your torso. Breathe in and pull your navel in tightly.

2. Point your toes and lift your legs to reach behind your head.

3. Breathing out, move slowly until your feet touch the mat behind your head.

4. Breathe in and then reverse the movement until your legs are vertical again.

Breathe in and repeat the whole exercise five to ten times.

5. Breathe out and spread your legs until your feet are level with your hands.

Single-leg Circle

An exercise for increasing core strength and flexibility and strengthening the hip joint.

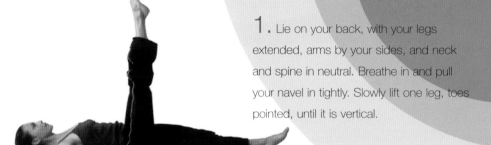

1. Lie on your back, with your legs extended, arms by your sides, and neck and spine in neutral. Breathe in and pull your navel in tightly. Slowly lift one leg, toes pointed, until it is vertical.

2. Breathe out and very gently make a circle with your toes.

3. Rotating from the hip, make five to ten circles in one direction, then breathe in again. As you breathe out, repeat, but this time moving in the opposite direction.

Remember to keep your pelvis flat and stationary throughout the exercise.

Single-leg Stretch

Another exercise to improve core and hip strength, as well as hip flexibility.

1. Lie on your back, with your spine and neck in neutral, knees bent, and feet on the floor. Breathe in and pull your navel in tightly, while pushing your spine against the floor. Lift your knees so that they rise vertically above your hips, return your spine to neutral, and make sure that your knees are bent at a right angle. Breathe out.

Repeat five to ten times for each leg.

2. Breathe in again. As you breathe out, slowly extend one leg, maintaining your spine and pelvis in neutral as you move. Once you reach the point at which your spine's neutral position is threatened, reverse the leg's movement, breathe in again, and, as you breathe out, extend the other leg. Make sure that you keep the stationary leg absolutely still, and that your hip and knee joints form right angles.

Double-leg Stretch

Core and back strength will be improved by this routine.

1. Lie on your back, with your spine and neck in neutral, knees bent, and feet on the floor. Breathe in and pull your navel in tightly. Push your spine against the floor.

2. Lift your knees so that they rise vertically above your hips, return your spine to neutral, and make sure that your knees remain bent in a right angle.

3. Breathe out and extend your legs, toes pointed, so that they form an angle of 45 degrees to the horizontal. Extend your arms so that they are parallel to your legs.

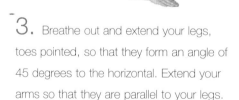

Return to the starting position and repeat five to ten times.

4. Breathe in. While breathing out, move your arms in a big circle over and behind your head, and then round them back, parallel to your legs.

Neck Pull

This exercise will strengthen and mobilize the core and back.

1. Lie on your back, with your legs extended and spine and neck in neutral. Place your hands behind your neck at the base of your skull.

2. Breathe in and pull your navel in tightly. As you breathe out, gently lift your head, shoulders, and back off the mat by rounding your spine and lifting each vertebra in turn.

3. Keeping your elbows in a "V" shape and pointing outward, continue until you have reached as far forward as you can go. Breathe and then reverse the movement until you are lying on the mat again.

Repeat five to ten times in total.

Spine Stretch

This routine will stretch the spine and hamstrings.

1. Sit tall on the mat, with your legs extended in front of you and your feet apart. Lift your arms to shoulder level, keeping them parallel to the mat.

2. Breathe in and pull your navel in tightly. Then, gently breathing out, lean forward from your hips, keeping your arms parallel to the mat and your neck and spine in neutral.

3. When you can no longer hold neutral, curve your spine forward while maintaining the arm position. When you are at the limit, gently round your arms down to the floor.

Breathe in and retrace the steps back to the start, lifting your arms first, then unrounding your back to neutral spine, and finally leaning back until your spine is vertical.

Shoulder Bridge

An exercise for improving core strength and control, as well as spinal mobility.

1. Lie on your mat, with your feet on the floor and knees bent. Place your arms by your sides and keep your neck and spine in neutral.

2. Breathe in, pull your navel in tightly, then tilt your pelvis toward the ceiling. While breathing out, lift your hips so that they are in line with an imaginary straight line connecting your shoulder and knee.

3. Keeping your hips level and your thighs parallel to one another, gently extend one leg at the knee.

4. Breathe in and raise your leg to a vertical position. Then breathe out and lower it, still extended, so that your knees are together again.

Repeat the lift five times. As you breathe in for the last time, lower your foot to the mat and gently round your spine, vertebra by vertebra, back onto the mat. Repeat the whole exercise for the other side.

Rocker With Open Legs

A routine to improve the strength of the core, the flexibility of the spine, and overall balance.

1. Sit on your mat, with both feet lifted above the ground in front of you, and find a balanced position. Hold your spine straight and in neutral. With your arms positioned inside your knees, grasp each ankle with the same-side hand.

2. Maintaining your balanced position, gently extend one leg.

4. Roll back on to your shoulder blades, keeping your legs and arms extended as you do so.

3. Then extend the other leg, keeping hold of your ankles. Gently round your lower spine, breathe in, and pull your navel in tightly in a controlled movement.

5. Breathe out and then reverse the roll, using your abdominal muscles to pull you back into a balanced position. Breathe in again and repeat five to ten times.

Bicycle *(Full)*

This exercise promotes balance control, core strength, and hip mobility.

1. Lie on your back, with your head and neck in neutral, your legs vertical, and your toes pointed. Breathe in and pull your navel in tightly.

2. Raise your hips and stretch your legs so that your toes are vertically above your face. Support your hips with your hands, with your elbows resting on the mat.

3. Breathe out, and then, breathing naturally, pedal one foot toward the mat, bending the knee as it reaches its fullest extent. Do the opposite with the other leg. Maintain your torso position and perform five repetitions with each leg in this direction, then reverse the direction for another five.

When you finish, take a breath, pull your navel in tightly, remove your hands from your hips, and control your spine as you roll it back down onto the mat.

Side Kick

This exercise is ideal for building core strength, especially the obliques and the muscles of the hips and thighs.

1. Lie on your side, with a hand supporting your head, your body forming a straight line from head to toe, and your hips stacked vertically, one on top of the other.

2. Breathe in and pull your navel in tightly. Lift both legs off the floor 4 to 6 inches (10–15 cm).

3. Breathe out and balance, then breathe in again and lift your top leg until it is level with your hip.

4. Stabilize your position, and then, breathing out gently, kick your top leg forward as far as you can while maintaining your balance. Breathe in again, and while breathing out, circle your leg three times in one direction. Breathe in, reverse the circle, then draw your leg back to your body.

Start the kick again and repeat for a total of five on each side.

Leg Pull *(Prone)*

This exercise will strengthen the shoulders and improve core strength, as well as stretching the muscles of the lower leg.

1. Start in the push-up position, with your arms extended directly beneath your shoulders.

2. Your shoulders, hips, and heels should form a straight line, bridging between your hands and toes. Your head, neck, and spine should be in neutral, with your elbows relaxed and hips held so that they neither sag nor lift.

3. Breathe in and pull your navel in tightly. As you breathe out, gently lift one leg (to help to keep everything aligned, think of it as lifting the heel of this foot). Keeping your hips and raised leg parallel to the floor, hold the position for a count of five.

Breathe in, lower your leg to the floor, then repeat for the other side. Repeat five times for each leg.

Leg Pull-up

This exercise strengthens the core, arms, and shoulders, and stretches the muscles of the front of the thigh.

1. Sit on your mat, with your feet extended in front of you and your hands on the mat behind you, with your fingers pointing forward.

2. Breathe in, pull your navel in tightly, and then lift your hips toward the ceiling, bringing them into a position in which they are in line with an imaginary line running from your shoulders to your heels.

3. Breathe out and lift your right leg toward the ceiling (think of this movement as being a lifting of the heel if this helps you to stay stable and balanced). Hold this position for a count of five.

Breathe in, and lower your heel to the mat. Breathing out, repeat with the other leg. Repeat five to ten times for each leg.

Jackknife

This exercise builds core strength.

1. Lie on your back on the mat, with your hands by your sides and legs extended. Keep your neck and spine in neutral.

2. Breathe in, and pull your navel in tightly. While breathing out, slowly lift your legs toward the ceiling. Round your spine upward, vertebra by vertebra, until your feet are vertically above your face and pointing at the ceiling.

3. When in the peak position, breathe in again, and, keeping your legs stretched and your feet above your face, round your spine back down onto the mat and then lower your legs to the mat.

Repeat five to ten times.

Swan Dive

This exercise helps to strengthen the core, back, arms, and legs.

1. Lie face down, legs extended. Place your hands underneath your shoulders and keep your neck and spine in neutral.

2. Breathe in and extend your arms as far as possible, pushing your chest and shoulders off the mat.

3. Breathe out and extend your arms at shoulder level at an angle of 30 degrees to your torso.

4. As you roll your chest onto the mat, tighten the muscles of your legs and back and lift your extended legs high behind you. Breathe in again and lift your chest and arms.

Repeat for a total of five times.

Double-leg Kick

An exercise to stretch the back and abdominals, as well as the back of the legs.

1. Lie on your mat on your stomach, with your hands clasped in the small of your back and your legs extended.

2. Keeping your hips on the mat and chin tucked in, lift your torso off the mat while maintaining your neck in neutral. Breathing out, extend your arms down your back, keeping your legs stretched out as far as you can.

3. Breathe in and pull your navel in tightly. Then kick both heels toward your bottom three times in quick succession.

4. Breathe out and return to the starting position. Repeat ten times.

Boomerang

This complex set of movements mobilizes the spine and uses the strength of the core to coordinate the body.

1. Sit on your mat, with your back held straight and your legs extended in front of you and crossed at the ankles. Breathe in and pull your navel in tightly.

2. Lean forward from your hips and counterbalance by moving your arms behind you. Gently roll back, keeping your legs stretched and at right angles to your torso. Use your arms for balance and support.

3. Breathe in and bring yourself back into a balanced position on your sitting bones, with your legs and arms held parallel at a 45-degree angle.

4. At the balance point, breathe again and recross your ankles.

5. Repeat ten times.

Swimming

An exercise to strengthen the shoulders and muscles of the back of the legs.

1. Kneel on all fours on your mat. Your knees should be directly in line with your hips, so that your thighbones are vertical, with your hands placed directly beneath your shoulders. Your spine and neck should be in neutral. Breathe in and pull your navel in tightly.

2. Gently stretch your right arm and left leg away from you as far as you can without tilting or rotating your hips or shoulders. Your leg should never rise above your hip and your arm should be level with your shoulder. Your torso should always remain parallel to the floor.

*Breathe out and lower,
then repeat for the other side.
Repeat ten times for each side.*

Crab

This routine enhances core strength and spine mobility.

1. Sit up straight at the front of your mat, balancing on your sitting bones and holding onto your crossed ankles. Breathe in and pull your navel in tightly.

2. Keeping your heels close to your thighs, gently round your spine and roll back onto the mat as far as your shoulder blades.

3. Breathe out as you roll back up into the balanced position, still keeping your heels close to your thighs. Keeping your feet off the floor, stretch your spine into neutral again.

Repeat five to ten times.

Control Balance

This exercise improves core strength and coordination.

1. Lie on your back on your mat, with your legs extended, arms by your sides, and head, neck, and spine in neutral.

2. Breathe in and pull your navel in tightly. Lift your legs, still extended, over your head until your toes touch the floor.

3. Take hold of your ankles with your hands.

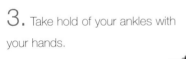

4. Breathe out and extend one leg toward the ceiling, holding the stationary ankle with both hands. Breathe in again and slowly change legs. Keep the movement continuous and flowing as you keep changing legs.

Raise each leg ten times in total, ending with the toes of both feet touching the ground behind your head. Breathe in and slowly roll your legs back onto the mat. Breathe out when you are lying flat again.

Scissors

Another exercise to improve core strength and spinal flexibility.

1. Lie on your mat on your back, with your legs extended and arms by your sides. Make sure that your head, neck, and spine are all in neutral.

2. Breathe in, pull your navel in tightly, and then raise your legs to a vertical position above your hips. Breathe out and use the core to lift your back and legs higher so that you are resting on your shoulder blades and your feet are positioned vertically above your face. Support your weight by putting your hands on your hips.

3. Breathe again and gently part your legs, moving them forward and backward in a scissor movement. Hold your torso steady and ensure that both legs move the same amount. (The tendency is to move one a lot more than the other, so be vigilant about this.) Repeat for ten movements each way, increasing the size of the movements as you gain strength and confidence.

4. When you finish, bring both legs together, breathe in, and gently reverse the movement, breathing out as you lower your legs back onto the mat.

Corkscrew

This exercise strengthens the core and back and increases the flexibility of the spine.

1. Lie on the mat on your back, with your legs extended and hands by your sides. Your head, neck, and spine should be in neutral. Breathe in and pull your navel in tightly.

2. Breathe out and slowly raise your legs (keeping them stretched) past your hips.

3. Then take them over your head, toward the floor.

4. Breathe in again, and as you breathe out, gently lower your hips sideways, toward the mat, at the same time extending your legs toward the floor.

5. Keeping control of the movement, gently rotate your feet in a big, clockwise circle. Breathe in again, and as you breathe out, reverse the movement so that you are moving in a counterclockwise direction.

Repeat for a total of ten in each direction, then breathe in and gently lower your legs to the floor, breathing out as you lie flat.

Hip Twist

1. Sit on the mat, your neck and back in neutral, chest lifted, and knees bent. Place your hands behind you, fingers facing forward and elbows relaxed. Lean back until you can feel your hip bones beneath you.

2. Breathe in and pull your navel in tightly as you gently extend your legs and lift them off the floor, making a "V" shape at the hips. Ensure that you keep your back long and chest lifted. Breathe out.

3. Breathe in again, tighten your navel, and keep your legs stretched out as you circle your feet in a clockwise direction, remembering that the movement is generated from the core.

4. After one circle, breathe, rebalance yourself, and make a circle in the opposite direction. Try to ensure that your shoulders and torso stay quite still. Repeat ten times.

Saw

This exercise stretches the obliques, the thighs, and the spine.

1. Sit on your mat, with your spine held straight and in neutral, and your arms extended to the sides and level with your shoulders. Extend your legs in front of you, with your feet flexed and about 24 inch (60 cm) apart.

2. Breathe in, and as you breathe out, slowly turn to one side from your waist. Everything below your waist should stay still, and your arms should not move in a different direction than your shoulders.

3. On your right side, reach across and down to hold the outside of your right foot.

Breathe in again as you lift yourself and rotate back into the starting position. Then breathe out as you turn in the opposite direction and repeat. Repeat five to ten times for each side.

Rocker

This exercise stretches the front of the thighs, shoulders, and arms, and strengthens the core and back.

1. Lie on your stomach on your mat, with your knees bent and your hands grasping your ankles.

2. Breathe in, pull your navel toward your spine, and then try to touch the back of your skull with your feet.

3. In this stretched position, rock forward onto your chest while breathing out. Breathe in again and rock back onto your thighs, using your ankles to pull you back and up.

Rock both ways ten times, then stretch out straight.

Swiss-ball Exercises

While not strictly Pilates, using a Swiss ball can add variety and challenge to a workout. Use it in conjunction with a Pilates mat program, and you can develop a truly all-round regime. Remember, however, that your brain is required to work, too, just as it is for Pilates.

Swiss-ball Exercises

Somewhat surprisingly, the Swiss ball first appeared during the 1930s in Italy, although its name suggests that it must have been used in the health spas of Switzerland at some stage. Today, you're increasingly likely to come across these physiotherapy balls in offices, clinics, and gyms. Training with one of these balls is great fun, as well as one of the most effective ways of providing yourself with a method of both developing and maintaining a functional core. In addition, the balls are available in all sizes and weights and are of varying quality, so that they can be adapted to suit most environments.

The importance of having a strong central core has been explained earlier in the book. The Swiss ball provides the opportunity to develop a creative, balanced exercise routine that takes us out of the single plane that most Pilates exercises employ. As well as developing and maintaining the core, such exercises require a great deal of coordination and general motor skills, and are therefore invaluable in promoting functional fitness.

In terms of usability, the ball has a number of advantages.

- Anybody of any age or fitness level, even if injured, can perform a program of exercises on the ball.
- The ball can be used equally effectively in a class setting or when exercising by yourself.
- The ball is invaluable in posture training since it encourages activation of the core and the lengthening of the spine into a neutral position, rather than spinal flexion, which is more usual when seated.
- Using the ball promotes core strength, which is vital for spinal health and daily activity.
- If used properly, and with a well-devised program, it can help to prevent injuries. Using a Swiss ball encourages movement in all three planes (horizontal, vertical, and diagonal) and through all of the ranges. In this way, joints are used as they are in everyday life, but with some measure of control and protection. Muscles can be strengthened without being exposed to impact or stress.
- The nervous system is also stimulated by the slightly unpredictable and unstable movements of the Swiss ball, which improves alertness and reaction times.
- When used properly and regularly, Swiss-ball exercises enhance the three definitions of fitness: muscular endurance, muscular strength, and mobility or flexibility.
- And perhaps the most important effect of using the ball is that it generates a huge increase in body awareness, balance, and coordination. This is important because it is due to this confidence that we are able to make progress and to achieve some of the harder physical activities on which the initial training is based.

For the Pilates student, these exercises are a very useful adjunct to the mat work that we have previously practiced. They move us up from the floor, use the core muscles that we have been developing, and make all of the exercises just that little bit more functional. I use a combination of mat work, Swiss ball, and gym and aerobic exercises to keep my overall fitness and development well balanced.

Using the Swiss Ball Safely

Exercising on a ball is a safe and effective way of working out. Nonetheless, as with any routine, there are risks, and it is therefore sensible to read and understand the precautions noted here before starting a program.

- The ball is made from a plastic-based material, so it is sensitive to extremes of temperature and sunlight. Ensure that you never store it or use it near radiators, fires, or hot lamps. By all means use it in direct sunlight, but store it somewhere where this will not be a problem.

- Make certain that the exercise space that you are using is big enough for you to move around on the ball. You need to be able to lie on it and roll on it, as well as sit on the ball, and furniture can be uncomfortably hard and sharp if you hit it! If you take the ball outside, the ground surface needs to be flat and level.

- Choose your footwear with care. Nonslip soles are vital in order to apply force to the floor from unexpected directions. Socks are not really suitable as they slip. I prefer to keep my feet bare. This has the added advantage that my feet are in direct contact with the floor, so that there is nothing to interfere with the flow of sensory information to the central nervous system.

- You need to wear comfortable clothing, ideally something that covers your arms and legs to avoid excessive friction on the skin, which can be uncomfortable. Make sure that your workout gear is not too loose, however, as loose clothing may be caught or twisted between you and the ball, causing you to lose your balance.

- Remember that the ball is made of a soft material that can easily be damaged by sharp or hard objects. Regularly check for any "bruising" by holding the ball up to the light and looking for any discoloration.

To inflate the ball, use any suitable pump. Ideally, this should be done at room temperature. Instructions should come with the ball saying how much "give" you should feel when it is fully inflated. Do not exceed this. In any event, the ball should reach the right height when the pressure is right, so this gives you a rough rule of thumb. Also take account of the maximum load indicated on the packaging. (Since it is usually in excess of 250 lb [113 kg], this is unlikely to be a problem for most people.)

- Although a stair landing may appear the perfect place for your workout, with plenty of space and no objects to impede free movement, do not be tempted to exercise here. The risk of falling down stairs may not be great, but it is significant.
- The ball will become dirty because it is made of plastic, and the static electricity that it generates attracts both dust and dirt. Use only the gentlest detergent and a very soft cloth when cleaning it.
- Bear in mind that the main purpose of using a ball is to encourage good posture. Try to capitalize on this by constantly thinking about the position of your spine while you are working out.
- If you feel dizzy or faint, or if you experience any pain or shortness of breath while exercising, stop immediately. Generally speaking, the ball is very safe to use, but if you fall off it, you may still hurt yourself.
- If you think that exercising with a ball might be fun, you need to make sure that the ball that you use is safe. This means ensuring that the ball is the right size for you and that you keep it properly inflated. The following table provides a rule of thumb for sizing:
    for heights under 5 t 2 in. (1.58 m), an 18 in. (45 cm) ball;
    for heights ranging from 5 ft 2 in. to 5 ft 8 in. (1.58 to 1.73 m), a 22 in. (55 cm) ball;
    for heights ranging from 5 ft 9 in. to 6 ft 3 in. (1.75 to 1.90 m), a 26 in. (65 cm) ball;
    for heights over 6 ft 3 in. (1.90 m), a 30 in. (75 cm) ball.

Warm-up Exercises

Just as with the mat exercises, you should start your program by warming up. The warm-up exercises on pages 62 to 77 cover everything that is required, so repeat those exercises, perhaps adding the following extra ones for the hips and pelvis.

1) Rotation

1. Sit in proper alignment on the ball, with your knees above your ankles and a hip-width apart, and your spine straight and in neutral.

2. Moving your hips only, and staying upright, gently rotate your hips in a circle, first to the left and then to the right.

3. Gradually increase the size of the circles and feel your waist loosening up. The ball should be rolling underneath you.

2) Lateral Shifts

Starting from the same position, and using your hips once more, gently push first to the left, and then to the right. As you warm up, gradually make the movements bigger. When you get to the maximum shift, perform about three or four swings to each side. Again, the ball should be moving underneath you.

3) Figure Eights

1. Now combine the previous two exercises and circle first in one direction.

2. Then move your hips slightly and circle the other way.

Stretches

The rationale for stretching is exactly the same as the one given in the mat-work section. Some of the stretches using the ball can be a little more difficult in terms of balance or positioning, however. If you find this to be the case, revert to the stretches given in the mat-work section until you feel more confident when working with the ball.

Back of Thighs *(Hamstring)* Stretch

1. Position yourself so that you are seated on the ball in an upright position. Push your feet forward and apart, so that your legs are extended and form a "V" shape. Lift your toes.

2. You may feel the stretch now. If not, keeping your spine in neutral, lean forward until you feel the stretch in the backs of your thighs. If you feel it behind your knees or in your calves, bend your knees slightly until the stretch moves to the backs of your thighs.

*Hold for five seconds and then relax.
Repeat three times.*

Front of Thighs
(Quadricep Muscles and Hip Flexor) Stretch

1. Start with one knee on the mat and the foot of the other leg on the floor in front of you. Position your hands on the floor, level with your front foot. Place the ball directly behind the knee on the mat.

2. Roll your back foot onto the ball and slowly force your knee back to the floor. Slowly bring your torso into an upright position. Now, pulling your navel toward your spine, tuck your pelvis under you. If you need more stretch, push your hips forward.

Hold for five seconds and change to the other side. Repeat three times for each side.

Chest *(Pectorals)* Stretch

This stretch can be an important aid to improving posture. As a result of the way that we sit at keyboards and steering wheels, the chest tends to become tight and the back muscles overstretched, so don't miss the opportunity to try this stretch.

1. Kneel on the mat with the ball in front of you. Place a forearm on the ball and roll it around so that your upper arm is at an angle of 180 degrees to your shoulder. Keep your shoulders parallel to the ground.

2. Drop your body forward, toward the ground, and feel the stretch in your chest.

Then adjust the angle of your arm and shoulder and find a new part of the muscle to stretch. Repeat three times on each side. Keep finding new bits of muscle to stretch by adjusting the angle of your arm until there are no more tight spots.

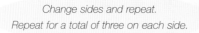

Change sides and repeat.
Repeat for a total of three on each side.

Shoulder *(Rear Deltoid and External Rotator)* Muscles

1. Kneel on the mat with the ball in front of you. Place an elbow on the ball.

2. Now pull your elbow across your body, rolling the ball and feeling the stretch. Push your elbow into the ball and try to pull your shoulder blade toward your spine. The stretch should increase in the back of the shoulder and the outside of the upper arm.

Hold for five seconds on each side. Then repeat, using a slightly different position for the arm and ball to stretch different parts of the muscle.

Abdominal-muscles Stretch

Be very careful when performing this stretch at first. If you feel at all dizzy, stop immediately because this may be a sign that the blood flow to the brain is being impeded. Consult your doctor immediately if this happens.

1. Start by sitting on the ball and then slowly "walk" forward, rounding your spine down, onto the ball.

2. Lie with your back on the ball. Get yourself into a position in which your head, neck, back, and all of your vertebrae are touching the ball. Extend your arms over your head. You should feel the stretch in your abdomen, and maybe also under your arms and through your ribs.

Slowly rock back and forth two or three times to feel the stretch in different places.

Side *(Oblique and Back)* Muscles

Groin Muscles

Sit on the ball. Keep one leg in place and move the other outward, to the side of the ball, fully extending it and rolling the ball slightly in its direction. Push your pelvis down toward the ground on this side. Make sure that you keep your leg extended. Now roll forward and back; do not bounce. Find each tight spot and hold your position for five seconds.

1. Extend your right arm so that it reaches above your head.

2. Stretch so that your right side forms a straight line from hand to foot.

Hold for five seconds, then change to the other side. Repeat twice more for each side.

Exercising

You will need to learn a couple of techniques before embarking on these exercises.

Lying on Your Stomach on the Ball

1. Start by kneeling behind the ball. Stretch your arms over it so that they reach the floor on the opposite side. (This will normally bring you into a position in which your chest is on the ball.)

2. Slowly "walk" your hands forward to bring yourself into a comfortable position in which the ball is resting on your hip bones and both hands and feet are in contact with the floor.

3. To get off the ball, simply reverse the procedure.

How to Get From Being Seated on the Ball to Lying on It

2. Round your lower spine toward the ball and gently "walk" your feet forward, away from the ball.

1. Start in the normal seated position. Bring your hands in front of you, keeping them low.

3. Allow the ball to roll under you as your back comes into contact with it.

4. "Walk" far enough so that your head and shoulders are resting comfortably on the ball. You can stabilize your position by lifting your hips and engaging your gluteus (bottom) muscles.

To return to a seated position, just "walk" your feet back, toward the ball. As your back rolls across the ball, use your abdominals to lift yourself up into a sitting position.

Try not to put your hands on the ball at any time because putting uneven pressure on the ball like this may cause it to become more unstable and slip out from under you.

The One Hundred

Using a ball can both reduce the intensity of this exercise and increase it. In other words, the Swiss ball significantly increases the range of possibilities for the exercise.

Beginner

Lie on the mat on your back, hands by your sides and spine in neutral. Put your calves on the ball, with your knees bent at 90-degree angles. The angle of your thighs and hips should also be 90 degrees. Breathe in and pull in your navel.

Hold for a count of five while breathing out through your mouth, and then in through your nose for a count of five.

Intermediate

Lie on the mat on your back, hands by your sides and spine in neutral. Put your calves on the ball, with your knees bent at 90-degree angles. The angle of your thighs and hips should also be 90 degrees. Gently push your heels away until you feel that the position of your spine or pelvis is being threatened. Breathe in and pull your navel toward your spine.

Hold for a count of five while breathing out through your mouth, and then in through your nose for a count of five.

Advanced

Lie on the mat on your back, hands by your sides and spine in neutral. Put your calves on the ball, with your knees bent at 90-degree angles. The angle of your thighs and hips should also be 90 degrees. Place the ball between your lower legs and hold it there. Breathe in and pull in your navel.

Hold for a count of five while breathing out through your mouth, and then in through your nose for a count of five.

Expert (Supine Lateral Ball Roll)

1. Lie with your head and shoulders on the ball and your heels below your knees. Lift your hips so that your thighs are parallel to the floor. Breathe in and pull your navel toward your spine. Extend your arms to the sides, level with your shoulders.

2. Keeping your shoulders and hips level and parallel to the floor, move crabwise to the left, lifting your left shoulder off the ball, but keeping your shoulders level with one another. Hold, count to five, and breathe.

3. Now move back in the opposite direction and hold for the other side.

Repeat three to five times for each side.

Single-leg Circles
Beginner

1. Lie on the mat on your back, hands by your sides and spine in neutral. Lift both knees to bring them vertically above your hips, with your knees at a 90-degree angle and your lower legs parallel to the floor. Rest your feet on the ball. Breathe in and pull in your navel. Take your right foot off the ball and make small clockwise circles with your right knee, keeping your hips and pelvis stable.

2. Breathe in for one circle and out for one circle.

3. Perform six circles in this direction, then six in the reverse direction, keeping the same breathing rhythm.

Change to the other leg and repeat the whole exercise. Perform three sets of each for each side.

Intermediate

1. Lie on the mat on your back, hands by your sides and spine in neutral. Lift both knees to bring them vertically above your hips, with your knees at a 90-degree angle and your lower legs parallel to the floor. Rest your feet on the ball. Breathe in and pull in your navel. Take your right foot off the ball and extend your leg so that your foot is pointing at the ceiling.

2. This time, circle the whole leg, from foot to hip, keeping your hips and pelvis stable.

3. Continue the exercise as described in steps 2 and 3 for beginners.

Single-leg Stretch
Beginner

1. Lie on the mat on your back, hands by your sides and spine in neutral. Lift your right knee to bring it vertically above your hip. Your knee should be bent at an angle of 90 degrees, with your lower leg parallel to the floor. Rest your foot on the ball. Breathe in and pull in your navel.

2. Gently push the ball away from you, keeping your spine neutral and abdomen tight. Breathe out as you push, and in as you pull the ball back.

Repeat for a total of five times for each side.

Intermediate

1. Lie on the mat on your back, hands by your sides and spine in neutral. Lift both knees to bring them vertically above your hips at a 90-degree angle, lower legs parallel to the floor. Rest your feet on the ball. Breathe in and pull in your navel.

2. Take your left foot off the ball and gently extend your left leg at an angle of 45 degrees.

3. Breathe out as you extend your left leg. As you bring it back to the starting position, resting your foot on the ball, breathe in again.

Change legs and repeat for the other side. Perform five repetitions for each side.

Double-leg Stretch

1. Lie on the mat on your back, hands by your sides and spine in neutral. Lift both knees to bring them vertically above your hips at a 90-degree angle, with your lower legs parallel to the floor. Rest your feet on the ball. Breathe in and pull in your navel.

2. Slowly push your feet and the ball away from you, keeping your spine neutral and abdomen tight. At full extension, hold, and then gently pull your feet and the ball back, toward you, breathing out.

Repeat for five times in total.

Shoulder Bridge
Beginner (1)

1. Lie on the mat on your back, hands by your sides and spine in neutral. Lift both knees to bring them vertically above your hips at a 90-degree angle, lower legs parallel to the floor and resting on the ball.

2. Breathe in and pull your navel in tightly. Gently lift your hips toward the ceiling while breathing out.

3. Hold at the top, breathe again, and reset your abdominals if necessary. Then gently round your spine down, making each vertebra touch the floor in turn, from top to bottom. Breathe in again, pull your navel toward your spine, and repeat.

Perform a total of five to ten repetitions.

Beginner (2)

Repeat the sequence given for Beginner (1), but this time keep your arms crossed over your chest. This exercise is considerably more difficult, so be careful that you do not fall off the ball. Repeat five to ten times.

Intermediate

1. Lie on the mat on your back, hands by your sides and spine in neutral. Lift both knees to bring them vertically above your hips at an angle of 90 degrees, with your lower legs parallel to the floor. Rest both feet on the ball. Breathe in and pull in your navel tightly.

2. Keeping only your feet on the ball, gently lift your hips toward the ceiling, extending them fully, and breathing out as you move.

3. Hold at the top, breathe again, reset your abdominals if necessary, then gently round your spine down, making each vertebra touch the floor in turn, from top to bottom. Breathe in again, pull your navel toward your spine, and repeat.

Repeat five to ten times.

Intermediate (2)

Repeat the sequence given for Intermediate (1), but this time keep your arms crossed over your chest. This exercise is considerably more difficult, so be careful that you do not fall off the ball. Repeat five to ten times.

Swimming
Beginner

1. Lie on the ball on your abdomen. Keep both feet on the floor. Make sure that your hands are directly beneath your shoulders. Breathe in and pull your navel in tightly.

2. Stretch out your right arm so that it is parallel to the floor. Turn your arm so that your thumb is pointing at the ceiling. Breathe out and lower your arm.

Repeat for the other side.
Repeat ten times for each side.

Intermediate

1. Lie on the ball on your abdomen. Keep both feet on the floor. Make sure that your hands are directly beneath your shoulders. Breathe in and pull your navel in tightly.

2. Stretch out your right arm and left leg parallel to the floor, with your arm at a 45-degree angle to your torso. Turn your arm so that your thumb is pointing at the ceiling. Activate the gluteus muscle in your left buttock by squeezing it as you stretch.

Hold at the top, then gently relax, breathe out, and lower. Repeat for the other side.

Advanced Level

1. Lie on the ball on your abdomen. Now walk your hands slightly farther away from the ball so that your feet lift off the ground and your hips and thighs rest on the ball. Feel your weight going through the ball. Keep your hands directly beneath your shoulders. Breathe in and pull your navel in tightly.

2. When you feel balanced, stretch one arm forward, at a 45-degree angle to your torso, with your thumb pointing at the ceiling.

Lower and repeat for the other side.
Repeat five times for each side.

Plank
Beginner (1)

1. Kneel on the mat behind the ball. Put your hands together (as if you were praying) on top of the ball, with your elbows resting on the ball beneath your shoulders.

2. There should be an angle of roughly 120 degrees between your torso and thighs and between your torso and upper arms. Breathe in and pull your navel in tightly. Hold the position and continue to breathe.

Hold for a count of twenty, then relax.
Repeat five times.

Beginner (2)

1. Kneel on the mat behind the ball. Put your hands together (as if you were praying) on top of the ball, with your elbows resting on the ball beneath your shoulders. There should be an angle of roughly 100 degrees between your torso and thighs and between your torso and upper arms. Breathe in and pull your navel in tightly.

2. Gently push your elbows and hips away from you, so that the ball moves away, too, and your body lengthens and flattens. Push as far as you can, holding your spine in neutral. Breathe out as you reach the apex point.

Hold for a count of one, then pull the ball back toward you, and pull your hips back, too. Breathe in as you move.

Intermediate

1. Place your elbows on the ball and your knees and toes on the mat. Your elbows should be directly below your shoulders. Breathe in and pull your navel in tightly.

Gently relax by lowering your knees to the floor. Repeat the whole exercise five times in total.

2. Slowly lift your hips toward the ceiling so that your body forms a bridge from your elbows to your toes. Hold, and continue to breathe normally for a count of twenty.

Leg-pull Prone
Beginner

1. Start with your elbows on the ball and your knees and toes on the mat. Your elbows should be directly below your shoulders. Breathe in and pull your navel in tightly.

2. Slowly lift your hips toward the ceiling so that your body forms a bridge from your elbows to your toes.

Hold for a count of ten, then lower your foot. Repeat for the other side. Repeat five times.

3. Continue breathing, and when you are balanced, keep your hips level and gently lift one foot off the floor.

Advanced

Repeat the beginner level to the stage of lifting one foot off the floor. Then, instead of holding it steady and in line with your body, move it to the side and hold. Repeat for the other side. Repeat for a total of five times.

Spine Twist
Beginner

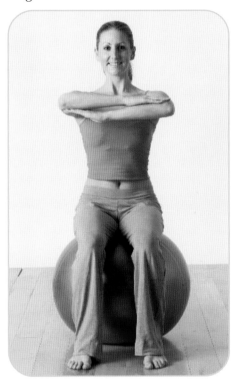

1. Sit on the ball. Ensure that your spine is in neutral, your feet and knees are a hip-width apart, and your knees are above your ankles. Breathe in and pull your navel in tightly. Fold your arms at shoulder level.

2. While breathing out, gently turn your torso to the right as far as you can without moving the ball. Make sure that it is only your torso that moves—everything else should remain in the same position.

Breathe in and turn back to the center. Then, breathing out again, turn to the left. Breathe in and turn back to the center. Repeat ten times for each side.

Intermediate

1. Repeat the exercise as outlined on the previous page, only this time, instead of folding your arms, stretch them out to the sides, level with your shoulders.

2. Again, as you rotate to the side, make sure that your arms move only with your torso, and not independently.

Repeat ten times for each side.

Spine Stretch
Beginner

1. Sit behind the ball, with your legs crossed. Your spine should be in neutral, your back and neck held straight. Extend your arms and rest your hands on the ball. Breathe in and pull your navel in tightly.

2. Lean forward from your hips, keeping your arms parallel with the floor and pushing the ball away from you, gently breathing out as you move. When you reach your limit, round your spine, including your neck, into a long "C" shape.

Hold for a count of two, then reverse the movements, straightening your spine first of all, then pulling back and bringing the ball with you into the starting position, breathing in as you move. Repeat for a total of ten times.

Intermediate

1. Sit behind the ball. Extend your legs, with your feet spread as far apart as is comfortably possible. You should still be able to maintain a neutral spine. If you cannot, either bend your knees a little or sit on a block or a pillow.

2. Repeat the exercise as described on the previous page.

Repeat for a total of ten times.

Side Kick
Beginner

1. Lie on your side on the mat. Make sure that your hips are stacked vertically, one on top of the other. Place the ball, ideally a smaller one than you normally use, between your ankles.

Then, breathing out, pull your leg and the ball back to the start. Repeat ten times, then roll over and switch sides.

2. Breathe in, pull your navel in tightly, then gently roll your top leg forward, taking the ball with it. Roll it as far as you can without compromising your balance.

Intermediate

This is definitely harder than the traditional mat version of the exercise, so make sure that you are able to perform the mat exercise before attempting this.

1. Lie on your side over the ball, with your hip and waist resting on it. Support yourself with a hand and a foot on the floor. Make sure that your hips are vertical.

2. Hold your top leg parallel to the floor. Breathe in and pull your navel in tightly. Gently push your top leg forward as far as you can, maintaining your balance until the stretch in your hamstring interferes with the movement and causes you to tilt or

3. Then, breathing out, pull your leg back into the starting position. Repeat ten times, then roll over and switch sides.

Push-up

Many versions of the push-up can be performed with a Swiss ball. The following are examples, but are by no means an exhaustive list.

Beginner (1)

1. Kneel on the mat with the ball in front of you. Place your hands on the ball, keeping your thighs vertical and leaning forward from your hips.

2. Breathe in, pull your navel in tightly, and press your chest to the ball. As you push your shoulders and chest away from the ball, breathe out slowly.

Repeat ten times. Perform two or three sets while experimenting with the position of your hands so that you use different muscles in your chest, shoulders, and arms.

Intermediate

Instead of bending at the hips, stay on your knees and extend your back so that there is a straight line from your knees through your hips to your shoulders. Then repeat the exercise as outlined on the previous page.

Beginner (2)

1. Kneel on the mat behind the ball. Reach your arms over the ball and place your hands on the floor. Gently and slowly, walk your hands forward using small steps, so that your feet lift off the floor and your hips are balanced on the ball.

2. Holding your body rigid so that it moves like a seesaw, breathe in, pull your navel in tightly, and press your chest to the floor. Push your chest and shoulders away from the floor and slowly breathe out.

Repeat ten times. Perform two or three sets, experimenting with the position of your hands in order to use different muscles in your chest, shoulders, and arms.

Intermediate (1)

Get onto the ball as described in Beginner (2), step 1. This time, roll farther over the ball so that your knees, not your hips, are resting on the ball. Then, while holding your body rigid so that it moves like a seesaw, repeat the exercise as described on the previous page.

Intermediate (2)

1. Kneel behind the ball, with your hands on it and your feet in contact with the floor.

2. Breathe in, pull your navel in tightly, then take your full weight on your toes and hands. Breathe out as you adjust your balance until you feel comfortable.

Repeat ten times. Perform another couple of sets and experiment with your hand position to work different muscles in your arms, chest, and shoulders.

3. Then breathe in, pull your navel in tightly, and press your chest to the ball. Breathe out as you push your chest and shoulders back into the starting position.

Roll-up
Beginner

1. Sit up straight at the front of your mat, with your legs in front of you, knees bent, and feet on the floor. Hold the ball between your knees. Breathe in and pull your navel in tightly. Round your spine and hold on to your thighs.

2. Gently roll yourself down onto the mat. Roll to the point where your feet are about to lift off the floor, and then use your abdominals to pull yourself back into a sitting position.

Repeat around six times. As you practice, you should gradually find yourself rolling farther back. Once your shoulder blades are touching the mat, move on to the next level.

Intermediate (1)

1. Start in the same sitting position as described in step 1 on the previous page, but this time hold the ball in your hands. Breathe in and pull your navel in tightly. Round your spine.

2. Gently roll yourself down onto the mat. Roll to the point where your feet are about to lift off the floor, and then use your abdominals to pull yourself back into a sitting position.

Repeat around six times. As you practice, you should gradually find yourself rolling farther back. Once your shoulder blades are touching the mat, move on to the next level.

Intermediate (2)

1. Sit at the front of your mat, with your spine in neutral and legs extended in front of you. Place the ball on your shins and your hands on the ball. Breathe in and pull your navel in tightly. Round your spine.

2. Gently roll yourself all of the way down onto the mat. Keep your arms extended and roll the ball up your legs as you round down

3. As you place your head on the mat, position your neck in neutral and hold onto the ball as you swing your arms over your head so that the ball touches the floor.

4. As you lift yourself up, reverse the process. Breathe in, pull your navel in tightly, and keep hold of the ball as you move your arms in an arc above your face. When your arms are vertical, using your abdominals, lift your body into a sitting position. Then lower the ball to your legs, roll it to your toes, and continue to roll your arms over it, feeling the stretch in your spine and hamstrings.

Reach only as far as you can while holding your spine in neutral. At this point, breathe again and repeat the exercise. Two or three repetitions are enough to start with, but gradually add more as you grow stronger.

Swan Dive
Beginner

1. Kneel behind the ball and gently roll over it on your abdomen so that your feet are on the floor and your hands are on the other side of the ball. Take your hands off the floor and place them on either side of your head. Breathe in and pull your navel in tightly.

2. Extend your spine so that your head, shoulders, hips, and heels are all in line.

3. Keeping your spine and neck in neutral, bring your hands down alongside your body, and rotate your thumbs outward so that you feel a stretch in your shoulders or chest. Breathe in again and hold for five seconds.

Breathe out and lower your hands and head into the starting position. Hold for five seconds. Repeat twelve times.

Intermediate

Perform the exercise as outlined on the previous page, but this time keep your hands by your ears throughout the entire exercise.

Upper-body Russian Twist

1. Use the technique outlined on page 171 to get your head and shoulders onto the ball.

2. Clasp your hands together and extend your arms toward the ceiling. Keep your hips high and parallel to the floor, and your knees at an angle of 90 degrees.

3. Rotate the ball underneath you by turning your torso to one side.

Now rotate the other way. Keep rotating from side to side until you have completed twelve repetitions for each side.

You can make this exercise more difficult as you grow stronger by first increasing the speed at which you rotate, and then by holding a weight as you rotate.

Lower-body Russian Twist

1. Lie on your back, with your feet on the ball and your knees at an angle of 90 degrees. Hold your arms out to the sides, level with your shoulders. Breathe in and pull your navel in tightly.

2. Slowly rotate your legs to one side, keeping both shoulders on the floor and maintaining an angle of 90 degrees at your hips and knees. Breathe, and then rotate your legs back to a vertical position.

Repeat for the other side.
Repeat for a total of twelve for each side.

Two-legged Bridge With Knee Flexion

Beginner

1. Lie on your back, with your arms held out to the sides. Rest your lower legs on the ball, knees straight, but relaxed.

2. Breathe in and pull your navel in tightly. Gently lift your hips toward the ceiling while breathing out. When your ankles, knees, hips, and shoulders are in a straight line, pull the ball toward you by bending your knees.

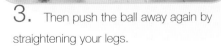

3. Then push the ball away again by straightening your legs.

Repeat twelve times.

Intermediate (1)

Perform the exercise as described on the previous page, but don't return to the floor until you have completed all of the repetitions.

Intermediate (2)

Perform the exercise as described on page 209, but keep one leg in the air and one leg on the ball.

Prone Hip Extension
Beginner

1. Position yourself so that you are lying face down over the ball. Try to make sure that your weight is supported by the ball, and not by your arms and legs.

When your thigh is level with your hip, return to the start and repeat twelve times.

2. Using the muscles in your bottom, raise one leg toward the ceiling. Keep your spine in neutral and navel pulled in tightly.

Intermediate

1. Position yourself so that you are lying face down over the ball. Try to make sure that your weight is

2. Extend both legs and raise them to hip level using the muscles of your bottom (gluteus) and those at the rear of your thighs (hamstrings).

Supine Hip Extension
Beginner

1. Lie on your back, with your head and shoulders on the ball. Start with your hips held high and your feet directly beneath your knees. Breathe in and pull your navel in tightly.

2. Lower your hips toward the floor, keeping your lower legs vertical and your head and shoulders on the ball until your knees are fully bent. Slowly breathing out, press through your heels and push up your hips into the starting position.

Reposition yourself if necessary and repeat twelve times.

Intermediate

1. Perform the exercise as outlined above, but with one foot lifted off the floor.

2. Ensure that you keep your hips parallel to the floor at all times.

3. Perform twelve repetitions for each leg.

Forward Ball Roll
Beginner

1. Kneel behind the ball, with your forearms resting on it. There should be an angle of about 100 degrees between your hips and torso and upper arms and torso. Breathe in and pull your navel in tightly. Hold your neck and spine in neutral.

2. Moving your hips and arms together, push the ball away from you until the point at which you are about to lose the neutral curve in the small of your back. Hold for a count of three, then pull the ball back to the starting position. Repeat twelve times.

Intermediate

Start the exercise as described above, but bring the ball closer to you, so that your hands and arms are lower down the ball.

Advanced

This is an advanced exercise. Do not attempt it unless you are strong.

1. Instead of kneeling on the floor behind the ball, start in the bridge position, with your toes on the floor and forearms on the ball.

2. Hold your spine and neck in neutral, with your ankles, knees, hips, and shoulders all in one line.

3. Breathe in and pull your navel in tightly.

4. Gently push the ball away from you by extending your arms.

5. Push as far as you can while maintaining your spine in neutral, then hold for a count of three.

6. Pull the ball back into the starting position and repeat twelve times.

Expert (For the Very Strong)

Start as described for the beginner's level on page 215. This time, however, place one arm on the ball and hold the other behind your back. Be careful when performing this exercise: it is very hard, and you need to be sure that your technique is good. Repeat the routine twelve times for each arm.

As you grow stronger, work through all of the versions for two arms using just one.

Prone Ball Roll
Beginner

1. Kneel behind the ball and rest your chest on top of it. Hug the ball. Breathe in and pull your navel in tightly.

2. Slowly roll to one side, keeping both knees on the floor. Hold for a count of three.

3. Breathe, roll over to the other side, and repeat.

*As you improve, roll farther.
Repeat twelve times.*

Intermediate

1. Instead of kneeling on the floor behind the ball, start in the bridge position, with your toes on the floor and your forearms on the ball. Hold your spine and neck in neutral, with your ankles, knees, hips, and shoulders all in one line. Breathe in and pull your navel in tightly.

2. Slowly roll to one side, keeping both feet on the floor. Hold for a count of three.

As you improve, roll farther. Repeat twelve times.

3. Breathe, roll over to the other side, and repeat.

Prone Jackknife
Beginner

1. Start by lying over the ball on your front, with your shins on the ball and your hands and arms supporting your weight. Hold your neck and spine in neutral. Breathe in and pull your navel in tightly.

2. Roll the ball toward you by bringing your knees under your body.

3. Make sure that you keep your hips low and your back straight. Breathe, and then push the ball back.

Repeat twelve times.

Intermediate

Perform the exercise as outlined on the previous page, then gradually move the ball farther away at the start, until you are resting your toes on it.

Advanced

Do not attempt this exercise until you can perform the intermediate level. Perform the exercise with one foot on the ball and the other held parallel to the floor.

Pilates During Pregnancy

You likely will not be a mother for quite some time, if that is something you aspire to, but if and when you become pregnant years from now, you will not have to abandon your Pilates routine. There are dozens of Pilates exercises that are safe to perform— and good for your health and well-being—when you are expecting and even far into your pregnancy. If your mother is expecting again, you can share these exercises with her and be her exercise partner, working out side by side.

Pilates in Pregnancy

While it is true that being pregnant does not make you an invalid, it is a condition that requires you to take care when exercising. The usual medical advice is that you should not start a new exercise program once you are pregnant, and that you should adapt the program that you have been doing once you know that you are pregnant. All of the evidence suggests that this is very sound advice, so the programs that I am suggesting here are for those who have already started Pilates before becoming pregnant. Consult your doctor about your desired exercise program to ensure that you can continue.

I have not listed all of the major and minor problems and complications with exercise that can occur during pregnancy because I believe that you should consult your doctor about anything unusual that you experience when you are pregnant. Never just assume that everything will be alright: it's important to receive medical reassurance and advice.

In addition, it will pay to take extra care in the following areas when exercising.

- Don't become too hot because the fetus is very sensitive to temperature.
- Don't overstretch. The hormone relaxin is produced during pregnancy to allow the joints to expand slightly, so be aware of your posture and the extent to which you are stretching. Overstretching is potentially harmful.
- However strong you are, do not be tempted to perform exercises that require you to raise both legs together at full stretch. You cannot afford to hurt your back, and this movement is very hard on the back muscles, especially now that your spine has more flexibility.
- Always move slowly. Your blood pressure needs time to respond to your movements, and nature takes care of the baby before it takes care of you, so that overexertion may leave you feeling dizzy or breathless. Moving in a slow and controlled manner is the best way—it's also the Pilates way.
- Never perform an exercise if it causes you to feel pain. Stop immediately and move on to something else. If the pain surprises you, consult your doctor.

Despite all of these injunctions, exercising during pregnancy is worthwhile and has many benefits.

- You'll sleep and relax better, and will therefore feel more energetic.
- Because your stamina will increase, you won't feel as exhausted as you may otherwise.
- Your circulation will improve, which can be helpful in preventing varicose veins.
- Your posture will improve, which, in a general way, will help you to avoid suffering from minor aches, pains, and discomfort.
- Your abdominal strength will increase, which, provided that your posture is correct, will protect the spine and support the uterus.
- Other things being equal, you should recover more quickly postnatally.

Warm-up and Stretch

Stand in a good posture, with your feet parallel and a hip-width apart.

1. Your weight should be evenly distributed between your heels and toes.

2. Draw in your navel and lengthen your spine, imagining that your breastbone is being lifted toward the ceiling.

3. Make your shoulders as wide as you can.

4. Now lengthen your neck, imagining that your skull is being pulled up to the ceiling.

5. You should feel as though weight is being lifted off your spine and is being supported by your abdominal muscles. Practice this throughout the day, and it should ease any proneness to backache.

Warm up by walking in place, then lifting your knees a little higher. Vary the direction by stepping backward and forward and from side to side. Keep going for about five minutes, until you are out of breath, but not completely breathless, and not too hot. If you experience any discomfort, stop until you feel better. If it persists, stop altogether, and if you are worried, consult your doctor.

Now that you are warm, start a gentle stretch. Remember that because of the hormonal changes in your body, all stretching needs to be gentle and controlled while you are pregnant, so always take care right from the start.

Chest Stretch

Stand in a good posture, as described on the previous page, then raise your arms to shoulder level, with your hands facing forward. Now try to reach behind you just enough that you feel a stretch in your chest and the front of your shoulders.

If you are tight in this area (and it is a vulnerability for some women), vary the stretch by altering the angle of your arm at the shoulder until you feel that all is released.

Cat Stretch

1. Kneel on the floor. Make sure that your knees are directly below your hips, and that your hands are below your shoulders. Relax your spine into neutral so that your head and neck are in line and your lower back has its usual curve.

2. Relax your back even farther so that the curve of the lower back increases and your spine is pushing toward the floor. Then breathe and push your spine the other way, rounding it toward the ceiling.

Hold this position, feeling the stretch, then reverse again. Repeat a couple of times until you feel freer.

Neck and Shoulder Stretch

Sit on a ball (or stand on the floor if this feels more comfortable) in a good posture. Keeping your head in its natural plane, tilt it to one side as far as you can, at the same time pushing the shoulder on your other side as low as you can. Allow the weight of the arm on the side to which you have tilted your head to rest on the side of your head to extend the stretch.

Remove your hand, turn your head to look at the floor, and now place the same hand as before on the back of your skull to feel the stretch in the side of your neck and into your shoulder.

Stand in a good posture, move one arm alongside your head and the other down your thigh, and then gently stretch your hands vertically away from one another.

Feel the stretch in your shoulders and neck. Hold for ten to fifteen seconds and then swap sides.

Arm Stretch

Stand with your feet a hip-width apart and raise your arms to shoulder height. Push the heels of your hands away from you and bend your wrists so that your palms are vertical. Hold the stretch for five seconds, then relax. Repeat two more times.

To increase the range of the stretch, keep your arms stretched wide apart and make golf ball–sized circles with your hands, first in one direction, then in the other.

Exercising

Some of these exercises require you to lie on your stomach or back. If you find the former uncomfortable, don't do it, and certainly not after the first few weeks of pregnancy. And if lying on your back becomes increasingly uncomfortable, find an alternative position.

Roll-down

This exercise warms up the back and loosens the spine in flexion. If you have a back problem, it will give you an indication of whether you will experience pain while exercising, enabling you to take special care when performing those exercises that put the back at risk.

1. Stand in a good posture. Breathe in and pull your navel in tightly.

2. Bring your chin to your chest, and, letting your head and hands hang heavy, slowly round your spine from top to bottom so that your hands are lowered gently to the floor. Keep your knees relaxed and try to keep your bottom still. Breathe out slowly as you descend.

3. At the bottom, breathe, and then curve your spine back up again.

Repeat the whole up-and-down movement three or four times.

Push-up

1. Kneel on all fours on the mat, spine and neck in neutral. Your hands should be level with your shoulders, but slightly wider apart, and your knees directly below your hips. Breathe in and pull your navel in tightly.

2. Resist the move as you make it, and press your chest to the mat, keeping your neck neutral. At the bottom of the move, breathe out and push your chest away from the mat. Resist the move again.

Swimming *(Kneeling)*

Repeat ten times.

1. Kneel on all fours on your mat, with your knees directly in line with your hips, so that your thighbones are vertical, and your hands directly beneath your shoulders. Your spine and neck should be in neutral. Breathe in and pull your navel in tightly.

2. Gently stretch out your right arm level with your shoulder, and your left leg level with your hip, as far as you can without tilting or rotating your hips or shoulders. Your torso should remain parallel to the floor.

Breathe out, lower, and repeat for the other side. Repeat ten times each side.

Roll-back

1. Sit up straight on your mat, with your knees bent and your feet on the floor. Breathe in and pull your navel in tightly.

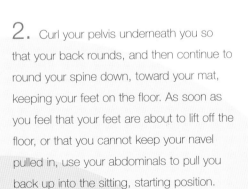

2. Curl your pelvis underneath you so that your back rounds, and then continue to round your spine down, toward your mat, keeping your feet on the floor. As soon as you feel that your feet are about to lift off the floor, or that you cannot keep your navel pulled in, use your abdominals to pull you back up into the sitting, starting position.

Repeat ten times.

Single-leg Circles

1. Lie on your back on the mat, with your arms by your sides and legs extended, and your head, neck, and spine in neutral.

2. Lift your right leg so that your knee is directly above your hip and your lower leg is parallel to the floor.

3. Breathe out. Breathe in and pull your navel in tightly again. As you breathe out, draw five clockwise circles with your knee, keeping your hips, pelvis, and spine absolutely stationary.

4. Breathe in again, and as you breathe out, draw five circles with your knee, this time in the opposite direction. Think of your hip socket as the pivot from which the movement is being generated.

Remember to keep the circles even, and gradually make them a little bigger. Perform up to ten circles, two or three times in each direction, with each leg.

One Hundred

1. Lie on your back on your mat, your neck and spine in neutral, and your arms by your sides. If you need to, use a folded towel to support your neck in neutral.

2. Round your spine against the mat, then lift first one leg, and then the other, into a position in which your knees are over your hips and your shins are parallel to the floor. Relax your spine into neutral again. Breathe in and pull your navel in tightly. Hold the position for a count of one hundred, breathing in for five beats, and out for five beats.

Keep your spine and neck in neutral at all times. If you feel that you cannot, rest for a while and then start again. At the end, gently lower your feet to the mat. Repeat three times.

Plank

1. Lie on the mat, with your elbows directly below your shoulders, and your forearms resting flat on the floor.

2. Breathe in and pull your navel in tightly.

3. Keeping your spine and neck in neutral, and your knees on the floor, lift your hips so that they rise just high enough to meet the imaginary line running between your shoulders and knees.

4. Keep your shoulders relaxed and your abdomen tight. Continue to breathe.

5. Hold for a count of ten, then gently lower your hips into the starting position.

6. Repeat three to five times.

Side Lift

1. Lie on your side, with your legs stretched, but not overextended. Your hips should be stacked vertically, one on top of the other. Your spine should be in neutral, with your head resting on your lower arm. Rest your upper hand on the floor, just in front of your navel, to help you to balance.

2. Breathe in and pull your navel in tightly. Keeping both legs together, lift your lower foot as high as you can off the floor while still maintaining your balance, and then breathe out.

Lower your legs until they are not quite touching the floor, and breathe in. Repeat the exercise ten times, then turn over and do the same on the other side.

Single-leg Stretch

1. Lie on your back on the mat, with your neck and spine in neutral.

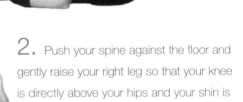

2. Push your spine against the floor and gently raise your right leg so that your knee is directly above your hips and your shin is parallel to the floor.

3. Relax your spine into neutral, breathe in, and pull your navel in tightly. Gently push your right knee away from you, keeping the left one absolutely still. Breathe out and bring your right knee back again.

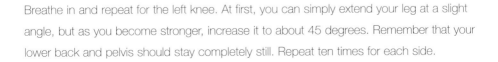

Breathe in and repeat for the left knee. At first, you can simply extend your leg at a slight angle, but as you become stronger, increase it to about 45 degrees. Remember that your lower back and pelvis should stay completely still. Repeat ten times for each side.

Shoulder Bridge

1. Lie on your back, with your spine and neck in neutral, your knees bent, and your feet on the floor.

2. Breathe in, pull your navel in tightly, then tilt your pelvis toward the ceiling and lift your hips while uncurling your spine from the mat and breathing out. Once you regain neutral spine, you have lifted your hips high enough. Breathe again, and move your hands in a semicircle so that they rest behind your head on the floor.

Breathe out and bring your hands beside your hips again. Breathe in as you hold the position, keeping your hips parallel to the floor. Then, breathing out, gently lower your hips to the floor by rounding your spine, vertebra by vertebra, back onto the mat. Repeat ten times.

Side Kick

1. Lie on your side, with your legs stretched, but not overextended. Your hips should be stacked vertically, one on top of the other. Your spine should be in neutral, your head resting on your lower arm. Rest your upper hand on the floor, just in front of your navel, to help you to balance.

2. Breathe in and pull your navel in tightly. Slightly lift both legs, breathe out, and hold. Breathe in and pull your navel in tightly again, then lift the top leg until it is level with your hip.

3. Then, breathing out, push your leg forward as far as you can while still maintaining your balance and the alignment of your neck and spine. Breathe in and repeat the kick. Try to increase the range of movement as you perform the repetitions.

Repeat ten times for each side. When you are stronger, progress to keeping your upper arm stretched alongside your body so that it does not support your balance.

Scissors

1. Lie on the mat on your back, with your spine in neutral, knees bent, and hands resting on your stomach. Your knees should be bent at an angle of about 90 degrees.

2. Breathe in and pull your navel in tightly. Keeping your hips and pelvis still, breathe out and raise one leg, maintaining the knee's 90-degree angle. Hold at the top and breathe in. Breathe out and lower your leg again until it is not quite touching the floor.

Repeat for the other leg.
Repeat five to ten times for each leg.

Spine Stretch

1. Sit on a ball, spine and neck in neutral, legs in front of you, and knees comfortably bent. Extend your arms softly, breathe in, and pull your navel in tightly.

2. Round your spine forward from your pelvis, toward your feet. Breathe in and hold at the full extent of the stretch, then return to the starting position while breathing out.

Repeat ten times.

Spine Twist

1. Sit on a ball, with your spine and neck in neutral, your legs in front of you, and your knees comfortably bent. Fold your arms across your chest.

2. Breathe in, pull your navel in tightly, then, breathing out, turn to the right as far as you can. Hold for a second, then breathe in and return to the start. Breathing out, turn to the other side and hold for a second. Breathe in and return to the start.

Repeat ten times.

Conclusion

Once your baby is born, do not be in too much of a rush to get back to exercising. If the birth was simple and straightforward, and you feel like it, you may be able to start again after about eight weeks, but you must not do so before at least six weeks have passed. Always ask your doctor's advice.

Your first postnatal exercises should be from the pregnancy program, and if they go well, try the beginner's exercises in the earlier chapters of this book. Again, the golden rule is to stop and go down a level if you experience any pain or discomfort, and if the difficulty persists, consult an exercise specialist, or preferably your doctor.

I would advise you to find a teacher or trainer for these sensitive weeks to make sure that you do nothing ill-advised and that your technique is good. As a parent of a new baby, you are likely to be sleep-deprived, fatigued, and anxious, which is why it's a good idea to get as much help as you can, even with your exercise program.

Machine Exercises

Just like any other exercise regime, Pilates can
be extended to be both more or less intensive
through the use of machines. Some teachers use
them for most of their pupils; others hardly
use them at all. Nevertheless, they definitely
have a role to play for the dedicated exerciser,
although they do take up quite a lot of space.

Machine Exercises

Many people first come across Pilates in studios in which a lot of exercises are taught using machines. These machines were originally invented by Pilates himself, and he called his (rather eccentric design) a "reformer." Like everything else in the world of exercise, his design has been adapted and changed to take account of shifting trends in fashion, tastes, and design, as well as new biomechanical considerations.

One of the most important changes is that it is now possible to manufacture these machines in a more compact and light-weight form than the originals. They are now often small enough to be stored beneath a bed or hung on a wall, so it is now possible to use this sort of equipment at home.

For the sake of completeness, some examples of the kinds of exercises that these machines are used for, and how they compare with the mat exercises, are included here. The machine that we used is called an Allegro.

The principles underlying the way that the machines (whatever they are called) work are the same. They consist of a flat "bed" or platform, which is moveable on runners and to which variable resistance can be applied by means of a number of springs. The exerciser lies or sits on the flat bed, and, using one or more of the specially designed attachments, works his or her arms or legs against the springs.

The major difference between exercise performed in this way and the mat or ball exercises described earlier is that there is usually an element of support on the reformer and the load is adjustable. Many of the exercises involve bodily movement (albeit only in the plane of movement of the bed), which can enhance how the core is worked.

This does not mean that machine exercises are any better than those performed on the mat. My own experience is that machines are the most useful for people with specific injuries (those who have suffered a stroke, for example), who can use the variability that the machines provide to focus on the area that they need to rehabilitate. They are useful for those who find particular movements and certain kinds of control a problem. In these circumstances, the teacher can use the machine as a tool to enable the student to feel the exercise without putting themselves at risk of injury. It also allows muscle and nerve connections to be made simply by repeating movements.

Exercising

Leg Circles

This exercise is a variation of one of the mat exercises; a comparatively new student or person with low muscle strength (but good coordination) can undertake a much more demanding exercise session using the machine.

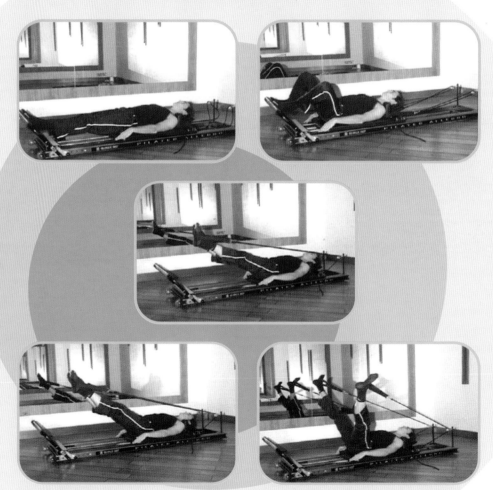

The Jackknife

Full and Short Spine Versions

Because the legs are supported to a greater or lesser extent, the jackknife can be performed on the machine with more certainty that the correct technique is being used than on the mat. This allows both teacher and student to be more adventurous and to progress a little faster than if only the mat were used.

The One Hundred

The version of the one hundred shown here is much more like the traditional mat version than that shown earlier in the book.

The machine supports the legs and head, which makes maintaining the spine in neutral slightly easier. The core can be tested more rigorously by varying the position of the legs and head.

This can be very useful if the primary objective of the program is rehabilitation from injury, as wider ranges of position may be used and the teacher can more easily gauge which everyday movements may be safely undertaken by the student. Using only a mat or ball routine can prove limiting and frustratingly slow in the early stages.

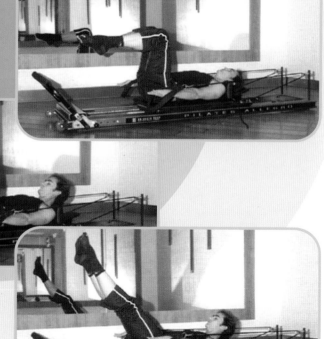

Triceps Press

This exercise is an example of how the versatility of the machine allows the teacher and student to be creative and produce new variations of the traditional exercises to suit the student's personal needs.

Here, the standard position for performing the one hundred is adapted to enable the triceps muscles at the back of the arms to be exercised, while still keeping the core active and spine and neck in neutral. Through the ropes-and-pulley system, the arms are required to move the seated student on the platform.

Resistance is supplied by the springing on the platform, which is variable. The student holds his or her spine and neck in neutral throughout, and controls the speed of the platform's movement.

The Flyer

This exercise tests the core while the student is seated, which is not easy to do using just the mat. The chest and shoulders are used to move the seated student on the platform through the ropes-and-pulley system. Resistance is supplied by the springing on the platform, and this is variable so that the intensity of the exercise can be altered. The student is required to hold the spine and neck in neutral throughout, and to control the speed of the platform's movement.

The Long Stretch

This exercise is akin to some of the exercises that substitute for the plank when using the Swiss ball. Once again, the student has to maintain the spine and neck in neutral at all times. The core is activated as the platform is pushed away from the handrest. The movement is more difficult than a mat exercise that, once mastered, is difficult to intensify. The core muscles and arms are required to move the seated student on the platform through the ropes-and-pulley system. Resistance is supplied by the springing on the platform; this is variable so that the intensity of the exercise can be altered.

The Offering

This is another exercise that tests the core and posture while seated. The shoulders and arms work against the springs in the equipment to move the platform and student's body weight. Resistance is supplied by the springing on the platform; this is variable so that the intensity of the exercise can be altered.

The Side Stretch

This exercise follows the same principle as the mat exercise with the same name. The springs and pulley system, coupled with the moveable platform, add intensity to the workout for the obliques, as well as an added level of complexity provided by the movement of the platform.

Conclusion

As you read these last words, you may feel as though you have been through something of an endurance marathon. If you have started a Pilates program, you should, however, already be reaping the health benefits.

These exercises really do deliver what they promise, making you look leaner and feel stronger and more flexible. As you continue with the program, other things should happen, too. As with all exercise programs, as you become more physically competent, your everyday confidence tends to increase, so that stress has less of a harmful effect on you, both physically and psychologically.

All of this also tends to make you feel a whole lot better, so that if you started off with a number of nagging aches and pains, they are probably less bothersome now. If the problems centered on your back or shoulders, you should be finding that the postural exercises are having an effect and that you are in less pain, or the pain is less intense. All in all, life should be better.

No exercise program can be complete or exhaustive, though, and those in this book are no exception. These exercises provide a very good basis for getting your joints and muscles generally fit and maintaining the appropriate level of fitness for you. They do not provide support for people with specialized needs, such as athletes or people with jobs that demand physical strength and skill, like firefighters or paramedics. If you fall into one of these categories, you need a specialist in exercise prescription (such as a personal trainer or physical therapist) to tailor a program to suit your needs.

Nor does the kind of regime advocated here include exercise of the type that will improve the function of the lungs and heart.

If you have been pleased with the results so far, you can improve them still further by beginning a cardiorespiratory program (provided that your doctor is in agreement) of walking, cycling, running, rowing, or using any of the complicated machines that health clubs keep for the purpose. But use your common sense when you start, and do not do too much too soon. Vary the activities and aim for three twenty-minute sessions a week, eventually increasing them to four or five.

If you can incorporate this part of your regime into your daily routine by walking, cycling, or running to or from work, you will soon become used to it and will miss it sorely if you have to interrupt your routine. In this way, you will be making all of your exercise functional, not simply part of some fashion trend. You will need little or nothing in the way of special equipment, and it will be cheap and easy to fulfill your program, regardless of whether you have to travel or not. You will be acquiring a level of fitness in a way that is enjoyable, that is suited to your way of life, and that makes you much more able to manage the stresses and strains that life imposes on you.

Lastly, if, having achieved all of this, you find that you are left wanting more, find a teacher of Pilates or of exercise in general. You will be amazed by how much more you can do when being instructed!

Index

Credits and Acknowledgements

Grateful thanks for all the patience and help of those around me during the writing of the book. Thanks to Peter Roberts, the Pilates teacher who demonstrated the machine exercises, and the KX Gym in Chelsea, London, who provided studio space for photography. The Swiss ball exercises were derived from Chek Institute levels one and two. Our thanks to our models Bladine Montagard, Jenny Tulloch, and Joy Worsley.

Bibliography

King, Michael. *Pure Pilates*.

Muirhead, Malcolm. *Total Pilates*.

Siler, Brooke. *The Pilates Body*.

Picture Credits